My MS Journey

Dear Sally —

Always recalculating —

All best wishes,
Judy Krum

Previously Published Books by Judith Krum

Gossamer Threads to Catch the Soul
Spiritual Reflections for the Church Year (2010)

In the Crayon Box, There is Peace (2012)

Softness for a Hard World
Poems and Photographs (2015)

Poetic Prisms (2017)

Color the Sky with Morning
Poems Inspired by the Psalms (2019)

My MS Journey
Recalculating

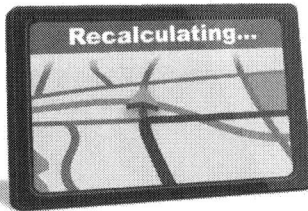

A Memoir by
Judith Krum

CHB Media, Publisher

ISBN: 9798985237429
LIBRARY OF CONGRESS CONTROL NUMBER: 2021924342

CHB MEDIA, PUBLISHER

(386) 957-4761
chbmedia@gmail.com
www.chbbooks.com

Cover Art by Koto Fega

CONTENTS

Preface

Life is not a straight line from birth to death. I wasn't born in 1942 with a prepaid ticket for my journey in the pocket of my footed pajamas. I didn't have a ticket to anywhere. That's the beauty of my story and everyone else's story. We don't know where we're going, and we have no idea how we will get there.

We look for signposts and markers along the way, hoping that these will direct us to family, happiness, satisfaction, and other good things. We hope the clues will help us avoid slogging through quicksand and bumping along undirected. Rather we hope the signs will show us routes to joyful miracles along the way.

But there are always bumps, pot holes, and detours. Who among us comes through life without scrapes and scratches, divorce, a diagnosis of a chronic illness, infertility and other contusions and wounds of body and heart and soul? I surely am not one of those who has escaped life's dents and difficulties. If you also have experienced life's ups and downs, then we have much common ground. How does my story mirror your story? Were you born with a ticket to a wonderful life already in hand? Or did you, like me, have to re-direct your course and map your journey as you bump into experience and recalculate.

Maybe one day I'll get it right. Having Multiple Sclerosis makes it almost impossible to plan a life, so every day brings a challenge of one sort or another. I keep trying to bring order to my life, but with MS, that ordering is nearly impossible. I keep having to recalculate to find a different route.

I have told my story as I remember it; memories can be imperfect. I have had several medications to help mediate my MS progression. Because MS is so different for each person, my story is not intended to promote any particular treatment or medical advice. Rather I tell how MS has affected me.

I was diagnosed with MS in 1985 at age 43, so I have been living with this chronic disease for 36 years. Over these years I have learned a great deal about MS, but, more importantly, I have learned how to make a life and to share it with others. MS has not been the only part of my life that has caused me to recalculate my journey. MS does not make you immune to other "slings and arrows" of life (to quote Hamlet). The first half of my life was probably quite similar to the lives of many others. I had loving parents, siblings, heritage from immigrant forebears, education, a career, a first marriage, travel, children, religious beliefs, hobbies, friends, and a passion for justice.

However, after my MS diagnosis, the second half of my life, while built on earlier values, has incorporated a new set of GPS markers that have recalculated my path many times. I have experienced loss and grief, joy and wonder, laughter and tears. I have become vulnerable. My hope is that people who read my story will understand that life can go on even though it cannot be completely planned and that it will have many signs for rough roads, pot holes, stop signs, yield signs, no U turns, and other indications of the need to recalculate. We just have to be aware of those signs and be willing to take the risks that are indicated.

Judith Krum, 2021

Carry Bags

My carry-bags are ready.
They hang on door knobs and on the back of my wheelchair.
They are hooked over hangers and floor lamp stands.
The bags are everywhere.
Ghosts and grime outline the logos and stitches of each bag,
And in some you will still find petals and conversations.
Food Giant totes and a Trader Joe canvas carry-all,
Crinkly plastic bags that once held onions and potatoes
and lemon yogurt,
The small bag I sewed and embroidered with redwork stitchery.
I cannot go traveling without the red one embossed
    with tiny white sheep and one black sheep,
The one from the gift shop at the Royal Botanical Gardens at Kew,
The one that has held crochet hooks and soft skeins of yarn,
Train tickets and hex wrenches.
The bag from Kew Gardens holds my walking days
    and forty years of my life before MS.
The sturdy purple bag with a zipper top
    is the one I use now for air travel.
The handle of that one fits over my head and around my neck
So my hands are free to roll and wheel
And hold the dog's carrier on my lap.
That purple bag came from a pharmaceutical company,
A free thank you gift for my prescription business.
But the red and white sheep bag is priceless;
It cost everything I had.

Chapter One
Carry Bags

Some people say that to tell a story well, one should start at the beginning. I have decided to begin with the turning point. I'd been forced to recalculate many times in my life prior to encountering MS, but this took recalculation to a new level.

That red Kew Gardens tote bag became the symbol of my walking days before Multiple Sclerosis. My Kew Gardens tote bag carries my walking days, the GPS of my journey from then to now, the map of 40 years of trial and error, of medications and research studies, from medical models to independent living paradigms.

My first awareness was the heat I experienced in England at Kew Gardens, and then, after I had been home for a few months, I woke up one morning in 1986 and was blind. All I knew was that I could only see one tiny peep hole through a curtain of black. I had to move the scene or the reading material or the TV show or the person's face if I wanted to see even a tiny, tiny bit of it in that one miniscule peep hole the size of a mustard seed. I was scared; I was horrified and desperate. No more driving, no more reading, no more writing. I would learn Braille.

At that time I was working as an English teacher and Guidance Director in a small high school in Vermont. Since I had been there since 1974, I knew my way around and, thank God, the students knew me well. Since my house was on her way to school, my colleague Nicky was able to pick me up before heading to school, about a 20 minute drive.

Wall-walking and measuring my steps, I got to my guidance office. I asked students what time it was. My first student counselee arrived at the office, and I asked her who she was and explained the difficulty I was having with my vision. She said, "Deborah," and I knew immediately who she was. With a senior class of only 37, I knew them all by name, voice, and reputation. I didn't have to do any writing, no forms to fill out or sign, just some personal discussion of Deborah's situation. I didn't need my vision for that, though I could sense her facial grimaces when she told me about the lack of running water at home and how she was not getting homework done on time because the kerosene heater didn't send any warmth to her bedroom on the second floor of their house.

When Nicky dropped me off back home after school, I called Dr. La Penta, my ophthalmologist, who sent me to Dr. Edwards, who would become my neurologist for the next 30 years. Dr. Edwards examined me and said that I had developed Optic Neuritis, which could be one of the first symptoms of multiple sclerosis. My questions and my concerns poured out. Would I be totally blind? Would I be paralyzed? Would I die? Was there a cure? Medications? Tests? What was next?

Dr. Edwards sent me to Dartmouth-Hitchcock Medical Center in Lebanon, New Hampshire, for diagnostic testing including an MRI. Indeed, when the results came back they showed the typical MS lesions in the brain and spinal cord. The exact cause of multiple sclerosis is unknown. It's believed to develop when the immune system mistakenly targets the substance, called myelin, covering your optic nerve (or other nerves), resulting in inflammation and damage to the myelin. Normally, the myelin helps electrical impulses travel quickly to the brain, where the electrical impulses are converted into visual or other information. Optic neuritis disrupts this process, affecting vision. These scarring lesions occur when the myelin sheath is eaten off the nerves by the body itself, causing disruptions in the electrical connections of the nerves. This is why each case of MS is different – because the disruption of nerves is different with each person. The MRI showed another problem for me — a pituitary adenoma, a small tumor of the pituitary gland which was causing excess prolactin to be produced. This is what had caused my infertility.

At this point I didn't know what would come next. Uncertainty and deep anxiety set in. Periods of weeping, of silence, of seeking the stories of others who had experienced similar conditions. Because I was sure I would remain blind, I began to research the programs and resources that were available to blind people. Could I learn Braille? Could I access books on tape? Could I afford to hire a driver or personal assistant? So many questions. So much to learn.

It seemed I didn't have time to feel sorry for myself; there was too much to do, and with limited sight, these tasks took so much time. With my one tiny peephole of sight, it took me hours to read just one page of text. And to accomplish this, I had to place the text on a well-lighted, flat surface just below my nose, slowly moving the text letter by letter and then mentally putting the letters together to make words and then sentences and then paragraphs. How long could I continue this way, trying to maintain my job as teacher and counselor, depending on colleagues for transportation?

My students were wonderful. They took me under their collective wings and helped me at school to get where I needed to be. They never took advantage, no practical jokes leading me to the wrong room or telling me incorrectly who was in the room or what time it was not! My blind life continued for six weeks, and then, as unexpectedly as it had begun, the blindness disappeared. It just went away, completely. It was a miracle! I could see again. I looked at text. I was able to read just like nothing had ever happened. No tiny peephole to see through. I went outside and could see the trees and the flowers and the cars going by the house. I got my car keys to open my car. I sat in the car for at least a half hour, sobbing with relief, and, I think, waiting for the blindness to return. But it didn't. I was astounded.

I called Dr. Edwards and asked him what had happened. He explained that the disappearance of blindness due to optic neuritis is typical after a few days or weeks or months. He reassured me that I would be okay and set me on a program of medications and therapy designed to build up my energy and try to slow the progression of the MS.

Multiple sclerosis is a disease in which your autoimmune system attacks the myelin sheath covering nerve fibers in your brain. In people with optic neuritis, the chance of developing multiple sclerosis after one episode of optic neuritis is about 50 percent over a lifetime. The risk of developing multiple sclerosis after optic neuritis increases further if an MRI scan shows lesions on your brain. So I was one of the lucky ones — both an episode of optic neuritis and an MRI that showed lesions on the brain. Dr. Edwards told me that there might be additional MS symptoms that would develop, things like foot drop, gait impairments, weakness, fatigue, cognitive disruptions, bladder and bowel symptoms. All of these symptoms would depend on which nerves were being attacked.

Becoming disabled as an adult is very different than being disabled from birth or in one's childhood. For more than half my life I had experienced life as a non-disabled person, TAB (temporarily able-bodied). Growing up and getting started on a career as a teacher prepared me for life as a non-disabled adult. I was privileged, educated, financially comfortable, now married to a man who loved me and whom I loved. The world was my oyster. I had a wonderful job in a small Vermont high school, terrific colleagues, students who were willing to learn and who responded to challenges. And then the second bomb hit. The first had been the diagnosis of infertility and then, in the mid-1980s, came the diagnosis of multiple sclerosis.

Dr. Edwards began to prescribe a number of new medications that were designed to slow the progression of MS. Over the years I have injected my thighs with Betaseron and have had injections of Avonex, either at the doctor's office or by my husband who was trained to administer those shots at home. I also had infusions of the steroid Solumedrol, usually every four months, in Dr. Edward's office. Solumedrol stimulated my nerves and was helpful in keeping me fairly active. My physical therapists became my best friends.

By 1990, MS had become part of who I was. My legs weakened. I was experiencing more foot drop of the right foot. I first used a cane for balance. Then I started using a Canadian crutch, also known as a Lofstrand crutch, a height adjustable crutch with an upper arm support cuff. My experience with this type of forearm crutch worked for several years as I maintained upper body and arm strength and mobility. I used one crutch on the right side so the crutch compensated for my lack of strength of the right leg.

Dr. Edwards prescribed a plastic orthotic for my right foot to help with foot drop and prevent me from catching my foot on uneven terrain and cracks in pavements. Getting that custom orthotic made was an experience in itself. I went to the shop on Ben Mont Avenue where their main business was providing mobility equipment like walkers and wheelchairs. The pedorthist only came to the shop on Tuesdays. I got to my appointment, and he put my right foot in a bucket of slimy plastic goo that was going to become a 3-D cast of my foot. Called a plaster slipper casting, this method applies plaster to the foot and then, once dry, it's pulled away from the foot to show the 3-D model. The cast model is then sent away to a lab where it is formed into the orthotic, using materials deemed right for my use. My orthotic was made from a rigid thermoplastic material which my pedorthist heated in an oven and with other heating devices to shape the orthotic. It was then cooled and trimmed and ground down to create a smooth finish. Then I tried it on and became acquainted with the Velcro straps that I would use to keep it in place. The final round was trying to fit it into my shoes.

I have large feet to begin with (in sixth grade I could wear my mother's size nine shoes) and now I had not only size eleven feet, but size eleven triple wide for my right foot. My left and my right feet needed different sized shoes. I couldn't afford to get two different sizes of every pair of shoes so I had to figure out how to make the triple wide left shoe smaller to fit that foot with no orthotic. How many kinds of Dr. Scholl's shoe pads are there? Well, I know of at least 15, all of which I tried in my left shoe to take up the slack space so that the shoe would stay on my foot. I tried massaging gel insoles, 16-hour insoles, air pillow insoles made of soft cushioning foam, dream walk fuzzy insoles, and many more. I put these in various combinations inside the left shoe to take up the excess space not needed because the custom orthotic was used in the right shoe only. With all of this *catoodle*, gone were the days of high heels. I had re-entered the era of Mary Janes and tied sneakers. I mourned the loss of pretty shoes that could match clothing outfits and that could be worn with dressy outfits and long dresses. I had a pair of raspberry suede heels that I had purchased back in 1973, and I refused to get rid of them. They were my very most favorite shoes, and I kept them until 2001. Just in case. In case of what? In case I suddenly no longer needed an orthotic. In case my legs were no longer weak. In case I could dance again. In case. In case. In case.

When two of my nieces got married, I had difficulty finding dresses that I would wear with my plastic orthotic and flat, rubber-soled Mary Janes. It just seemed that I was destined to wear jeans, capris, khakis and very casual clothing. Getting dressed up became harder and harder. Nothing looked good with my ugly shoes. When I began using a wheelchair, I thought I could go back to wearing nice shoes since I wouldn't have to worry about keeping the shoes on my feet. I wouldn't have to use the orthotic because I didn't have to be concerned about foot drop.

But I hadn't thought about getting in and out of a car or getting out of the wheelchair to use a restroom. My mantra became, "Nothing's easy." You just can't escape disappointments, at least I can't.

Not only did it become difficult to deal with clothing and shoes, but with an orthotic on my right foot, I could not drive. I worked with Vocational Rehabilitation to figure out ways that would enable me to continue to work. One of the most pressing concerns was the issue of transportation. Unlike major urban areas that have bus service, commuter trains, and other transportation infrastructure, southern Vermont does not have such possibilities available. The automobile is key to getting around on Vermont's two-lane roads.

Vocational Rehabilitation sent me to a driving school in Albany, New York, where I was to learn to drive using only my left foot. I had never heard of a "left foot accelerator," but that was just one of the new things that would help me to keep going as independently as possible. With the driving instructor in the passenger seat, I got into the driver's seat and surveyed equipment. The car was a Honda Civic similar to my car. It had two pedals—one was the brake and the other was the accelerator. The accelerator was outfitted with an extra pedal to the left of the original gas pedal and connected to the original pedal with a galvanized rod. There was enough room for my big, size 11 feet. I practiced moving my left foot from the gas pedal to the brake so that my muscle memory could write the new movement onto my brain. I practiced that movement for about a half hour before the instructor let me turn on the engine. We were going to drive around a small residential community first, giving me some time to get used to the new gas pedal arrangement and using my left foot.

I had gotten my first driver's license in New York when I was 21 years old and had graduated from college. My father had taken me to big parking lots and small residential areas to teach me driving skills far away from fast moving vehicles. And then, at age 46, I was being instructed in driving skills so I could keep my license and my employment. My instructor gave me confidence and assured me that in time, I would become very comfortable with my left foot accelerator. But it definitely took a great deal of concentration as I remembered that I was driving with my left foot. I could not keep up a coherent conversation while I was driving with my left foot. After a few sessions with the instructor on an instructional car, the left foot accelerator was installed on my car. And from that time forward, I was driving with my left foot.

I had to drive from Albany, New York, back to Vermont, a distance of about 35 miles. It was do or die! And I wasn't about to die so I had to do it. Concentration. No music on the radio. No conversation with my husband who had accompanied me. Nothing to distract me from remembering that my left foot was doing its job.

Chapter Two
The Welsh Dragon — More Recalculating
Travelers, not Tourists – Our second trip to England

BUT YOU HAVE MS!

I wasn't using a wheelchair yet and could still get around with crutch and orthotic.

Our friends and family were astonished that we were setting off on a vacation adventure with only our knowledge of the English language, a few tour books, a map of the British Isles. They peppered us with questions:

"You're doing what?"

"Do you have relatives in England?"

"How will you get around?"

"Are you going on a tour?"

We had made our own reservations at bed and breakfasts and English country house hotels, and were well supplied with an understanding of British culture, literature, music, and Anglican Church tradition. We felt much more prepared than our friends allowed.

We arrived at Heathrow on BOAC from the states and heard that unmistakable English accent. We were headed to England's West Country and to Wales. We took the train from London to Exeter. Chugging along on Brit Rail put us in the mindset of real English travelers.

The train stopped at the Exeter train station. We had pre-arranged for a rental car in Exeter. I sat with our suitcases and paraphernalia on the streetside of the station platform as I watched with sinking heart as Randy navigated across the tracks and the one block to the rental car garage. Thoughts raced through my mind. *What if the car isn't available? What if it isn't an automatic? What if I am to be stuck here on the platform all alone for eternity?* Other travelers stopped occasionally and asked if I was okay, or if I needed anything. Kindness was everywhere. I felt reassured.

In about an hour, Randy pulled up at the curb, smiling broadly from the right-hand driver's side of our rental car, ready to drive on the left side of the street. Again, our lives were turned backwards and upside down! Recalculating everything! Would we survive? Most of the work for our two-week trip had been done ahead of time.

RCI and Timeshares

After Randy's parents passed away in the 1980s, he received a bit of money and we discussed how best to utilize it. Since we both really wanted to travel as much as possible, we looked into the concept of timeshare purchases. As we drove north from Florida after the death of Randy's father, by happenstance we stopped at a roadside spot where timeshare purchases were being promoted. Because we tend to make decisions quickly and usually don't comparison shop, we listened to the 30-minute presentation from the timeshare salesman and purchased on the spot a timeshare at a new development on the Outer Banks of North Carolina. But it was the other travel possibilities that really sold us on this purchase. It was this quick decision to purchase a timeshare unit that led to our trip to the UK and Wales.

We could do what is called "exchanges" within the time share company and its member resorts. Setting the stage before we arrived at the rail station in Exeter and rented a car, the first exchange that we did was an exchange to a resort in St. David's, Wales, UK.

Earlier, in the late winter of 1988, we had reserved the time share exchange of a two-bedroom unit that came with all the linens and housewares that one would associate with a fully stocked home. After we had the timeshare date firmly set, I became the family travel agent. I bought a large print road atlas of all the roads and highways and cities and hamlets of the British Isles and set about mapping out a road trip for two weeks that summer. I had to determine how we would travel from Exeter to St. David's by way of Cornwall, through Land's End, Tintern Abbey, the Snowdonia Mountains of Wales, and along the craggy sea coast of Wales to St. David.

I also had purchased a small, 1986 paperback called *Country Inns and Back Roads: Country house Hotels, Bed and Breakfasts, Traditional Inns, Farmhouses, Guesthouses and Castles*. The book was a goldmine of information and contained lovely pen and ink drawings of the various establishments. The book even had phone numbers, names of proprietors, how to make reservations, (remember this was way before the internet, Google, and Kayak). There were tips on luggage, cancellations, air fares, rental cars and driving tips, dining in the British Isles, and information on London itself as well. Apparently I was not the first one to be doing this kind of search. From our Brit Rail station in Exeter, England, we started our trek, heading west toward Land's End in Cornwall from where Randy's family had emigrated.

The first place we stayed was the Mill End Hotel, in Chagford, Dartmoor, Devon. Everywhere in this lovely country house hotel there were scents of roses. Everywhere.

Besides the scent of roses, the hotel had an afternoon tea set up on the front lawn for all the residents. Once we registered and got freshened up, we went down to the lawn for High Tea. Fresh scones, strawberries, Devonshire clotted cream, accompanied steaming hot tea served in antique china cups with mismatched flatware. The lawns stretched out before us to give a sense of the wide expanse of the moor and the lovely adventures that lay ahead. We had dinner at the on-premises Mill End Restaurant and started to get acquainted with lamb and mushy peas.

After a full English breakfast the next morning, we set out for the Lamorna Cove Hotel, in Mousehole, Cornwall. Perched above the historic Lamorna Cove, the hotel was again a lovely place for relaxation. Randy set out on a hike along the legendary Cornwall coastal path while I was relegated to bed with a bad case of bronchitis. Although the bronchitis was getting worse and I was hacking a deep, mucous-lined cough, we had to set out the next morning for the next location. On the way we wanted to experience the mining industry of Cornwall. Tin and copper were the most significant metals mined in Cornwall. Driving from Mousehole and Lands End to Truro, we became very aware of the many derelict mine shafts that rose from the unforgiving rocky and scarred cliffs. When we arrived at the Poldark Mine, now a tourist attraction in Helston, Cornwall, we parked the car and I stayed in the car coughing and dozing while Randy took the tour of the mine.

Mining was the industry that kept most of the Cornish working class employed during the 1700s and early 1800s. Spending three-fourths of their lives underground picking away at veins of tin and copper, workers were often subject to black lung and other pulmonary diseases. Subsistence earnings also meant that starvation and deprivation were common. Long before labor regulations were considered, the miners were subject to the whims of the mine owners to keep the mines as safe as possible. There were many acci-

My MS Journey

dents as owners cut corners for profits rather than keeping the safety of their workers in the forefront. And even as tin and copper were extracted from the depths of the Cornwall land, there still remained the question of how to get the raw minerals to market. Protected harbors were needed for the transport of ore and these sites lay quite close to the Atlantic coast. Wealthy landowners attempted to construct safe harbors, but so often these efforts were dashed by storms and by greed.

From the 1820s, as Poldark-style veins ran out, the migration of capital and labor meant that Cornwall began not only to export its skilled workers, but also it developed a world-class export trade in mining machinery and technology. Cornishman Richard Trevithick developed a revolutionary high-pressure steam engine that was on the forefront of the worldwide expansion of the mining industry. Tin soon took over as top mineral. Production rapidly trebled before Cornwall hit "peak tin" around 1870. Then vast new discoveries in Australia, Bolivia, and Malaya made Cornwall's mining districts an early victim, having been a beneficiary, of the globalization of trade in natural resources.

Northwest of Truro, the village of St Agnes perches above the cliffs in a landscape scarred with mine workings and studded with engine houses. Soon, the coming of the railways to Cornwall would strip every remaining advantage from local seaborne trade.

As Poldark proves, enough time has now passed to transform the expenditure of cash, toil and human life in the Cornish mining industry from misery to myth. That myth describes the heyday of the Cornish mining industry in the eighteenth and nineteenth centuries: The metalliferous "mountain" of St Agnes has, it reports, yielded for more than 150 years "about ten thousand pounds worth of tin per annum." It keeps employed "about the same 1,000 persons, who for the most part spend their time in hard and dangerous labor in order to get a poor livelihood for themselves and families, in the pursuit of which, here and in other places, many of those poor men yearly by sad accidents lose their lives."

Those "sad accidents" forever scar the historical terrain behind the tourist fantasia. As in every mining region in the world, the photogenic stacks often stand guard over mass tombs. Sanitized and safety-checked, workplaces that weakened bodies, snatched lives and orphaned children in bulk now adorn a day trip. In the wake of the first BBC series in the mid-1970s, the old workings of Wheal Roots in the Wendron valley became a tourist attraction renamed the "Poldark Mine." The site now has a new owner, having passed through financial ups and downs that would probably not have surprised Ross Poldark and his kin.

Yet the home mines clung on tenaciously to a productive role. As late as October 1919, the tin industry could still deliver human disaster on a numbing scale. In that month, the crude lift or "man engine" that transported workers from surface to seam at the Levant mine near Land's End, collapsed. As The *Cornishman and Cornish Telegraph* recorded: "The tragedy was the work of an instant. Something snapped—perhaps an iron cap or bolt—and what has been described as a living pillar of men dropped down the man-engine shaft, crushing many to death, mangling more with the debris of breaking wood and metal."

In all, 31 miners died at Levant. With one eye on the global diaspora, the paper reported that "Cornishmen in foreign and colonial mining camps will read with unspeakable sorrow of this calamity." It launched an appeal for funds, listing the victims to indicate the level of their families' need. For example, John Tonkin of Boscean, aged 52, left a "Widow and seven children, three dependent". The Levant Mine is now a UK national Trust property, nestled within a Unesco World Heritage Site. *The Poldark Mine* is a tourist attraction near the town of Helston in Cornwall, England, UK. It lies within the Wendron Mining District of

Cornwall and West Devon.

Randy emerged from the depths of the Poldark Mine tour and came to the car to find me coughing and running a fever. We asked where the nearest pharmacy was and were directed to Truro. There the apothecary gave us some over the counter medicine that he said should help the coughing and the fever. Indeed, as we drove to the next stop, I began to feel better and was not coughing so much.

Lynmouth, North Devon, is a large town on the Bristol Channel, with Wales on the other side of the harbor. The rising and falling tides impacted the harbor so that when the tide went out, the boats in the harbor were stranded on mud flats, but when the tide came back in, the boats bobbed again in the harbor's waters. We were staying at The Rising Sun Hotel, a country house hotel made up of several cobbled together buildings with a thatched roof. Many steep and narrow stairways connected the various floors and hallways.

Our room was on the highest floor and from leaded windows it offered a panoramic view of the Bristol Channel and Lynmouth Harbor. There was an attached bathroom, a rare find in many English hostelries. And we were warned that flushing the toilet would result in very loud noises, not unlike the sounds of a lawnmower. Apparently, when the hotel underwent renovations, the water pressure and the sewer pipes in the bathroom in our room could not be completely modernized. Everything worked fine, but we nicknamed the toilet "the shredder," because it used a grinding mechanism to pulverize everything small enough to flow through the narrow, antique pipe system. Memories of the shredder and the thatched roof and the Lynmouth Harbor mud flats are still vivid.

The next day we drove into the Wye Valley on the northern side of the Bristol Channel to our next hotel. The

Crown at Whitebrook, Gwent, was an upscale hotel and restaurant, six miles from Monmouth and seven miles from the medieval ruins of Tintern Abbey. The hotel was a true village hotel, set by a brook that flowed into the River Wye. The gardens were filled with rhododendrons and roses, pansies and irises. It was set on the edge of Tintern Forest with its lush trees of ash, beech, and oak, providing homes for owls, nightingales and magpies. The entire area followed the hills and valleys along the River Wye. I could just imagine William Wordsworth with his sister Dorothy trekking along the River Wye in July of 1798 and coming upon the stone ruins of Tintern Abbey. On our visit, we found the crumbling stone an unusual mark on the verdant green of the forest. The skeleton arches and the fleshless ribs of the Abbey's remaining presence presented a stark contrast to *these steep woods and lofty cliffs, and this green pastoral landscape* of the Wye Valley. Much a Romantic, Wordsworth's lines resonate with me to this day.

Lines Composed a Few Miles above Tintern Abbey, On Revisiting the Banks of the Wye during a Tour July 13, 1798

By William Wordsworth

(Lines 28-50)

These beauteous forms,
Through a long absence, have not been to me
As is a landscape to a blind man's eye:
But oft, in lonely rooms, and 'mid the din
Of towns and cities, I have owed to them,
In hours of weariness, sensations sweet,
Felt in the blood, and felt along the heart;
And passing even into my purer mind
With tranquil restoration: — feelings too
Of unremembered pleasure: such, perhaps,

As have no slight or trivial influence
On that best portion of a good man's life,
His little, nameless, unremembered, acts
Of kindness and of love. Nor less, I trust,
To them I may have owed another gift,
Of aspect more sublime; that blessed mood,
In which the burthen of the mystery,
In which the heavy and the weary weight
Of all this unintelligible world,
Is lightened: — that serene and blessed mood,
In which the affections gently lead us on, —
Until, the breath of this corporeal frame
And even the motion of our human blood
Almost suspended, we are laid asleep
In body, and become a living soul:
While with an eye made quiet by the power
Of harmony, and the deep power of joy,
We see into the life of things . . .

This was July 1988. That evening at the Crown, I received a call from my younger sister through the hotel's master phone system.

"Judy," she said, "Dad died today." Through her shaky voice, I could feel the sadness, the strain, the terrible aloneness she was feeling.

"Oh, my God, Linda. What happened?" She struggled to tell me how he was out west visiting our sister Carolyn in Washington State, and he had a heart attack.

In that moment, Wordsworth's lines again came flooding back ro me:

For I have learned
To look on nature, not as in the hour
Of thoughtless youth, but hearing oftentimes
The still, sad music of humanity. (Lines 89-92)

The news of my father's death sent me into a spiral of sad uncertainty. Should we cut the trip short and head back to the United States immediately? Randy and I talked at length with my sister about what we should do. Linda said she had things in hand. Her husband Richard was helping her to get through the sadness. I was feeling very guilty. If we left and went back, there was still no time to say good-bye to him. Besides feeling sad for my dad's passing and for not being there to help my sister, I was very sad at the thought of not completing our trip that we had put so much planning into. No matter what decision we made, "the still sad music of humanity" was playing over and over in my head. We made the terrible decision to stay in the UK. Unfortunately, this left all of the hard decisions about Dad's funeral arrangements up to Linda.

All the tears and stress did not help my health. I could only think of my poor sister arranging Dad's funeral and burial through White's Funeral Home in Farmingdale, the same funeral home my dad had worked with when his wife, my mother, died of breast cancer in 1968. My dad had arranged for his burial in a cemetery plot next to my mother. And there would be flowers and there would be visiting hours. And I wouldn't be there. I felt I was letting my sister down.

Linda has been my best friend all my life. And to not be there at this time just about did me in.

Dad had lived in the house at 22 Pinehurst with my sister and her family ever since my mom had died. Linda had been his caretaker through hip replacements and other health concerns. I had been off living my own life, visiting once in a while but not putting in the hard work of caring for our dad. I felt very selfish. There was nothing else to say or to do.

We departed the Crown the next morning, after one final call to my sister. We were in Wales and heading north along the spine of the Snowdonia National Park on the two-lane carriageway (roadway), the A470. Except for the great numbers of sheep and the derelict slate and tin mining operations and the dual-language (Welsh-English) signposts, we could have been driving the route across southern Vermont from Bennington to Brattleboro on Vermont Route 9 — the Molly Stark Byway. In southern Vermont, there are the Green Mountains; in Wales, there is Snowdonia. There were no passing lanes on the A470, just small pull off areas, where a car or truck could allow for another vehicle to go past. The roadway was steep and narrow. For me it was a white-knuckle ride. I swear I said the rosary and the Hail Mary at least every five minutes during our trip through the Snowdonia National Park.

We were booked to stay at the Bwlch-y-fedwen Country House Hotel, Penmorfa, Porthmadog. The proprietors were expecting us and gave us an initial tour of the old coaching inn which dates back to 1664. Huge stone fireplaces, oak beams, antique furniture, and candlelight in the dining room and bar gave us a sense of the historic significance of this inn and the warm and friendly atmosphere we experienced. Typical of all the places we stayed, the Bwlch-y-fedwen provided a lovely connection to the people of the community and a place to relax and gather our thoughts. Most of the places we stayed had dining rooms/restaurants attached and usually the food was spectacular. Breakfasts were "full English breakfasts" of eggs, rashers of bacon, sausages, kippers, toast, grilled tomatoes and mushrooms, and pots of tea. Dinners were often house specialties such as roast lamb, roast beef, grilled fish such as plaice (flounder), boiled potatoes, peas, and sometimes root vegetables such as turnips, carrots, and beets. Home baked breads and cakes as well as desserts like the Queen of Puddings and a Victoria Sandwich (cookie/cake) were plentiful. Definitely, we concluded, you get to know the locals though their food. In all our travels, we never went away hungry or disappointed,

From our stay at the Bwlch-y-fedwen in the northeast area of Wales and just outside Snowdonia National Park, we drove south along the coast of the Irish Sea. One notable respite was at the equivalent of an American Truck Stop where we were in search of rest rooms, lunch, and coffee.

Even in such an ordinary stop, people were friendly and the food was good. It was here that we found out that "mushy" peas are indeed a real thing. Menus list Mushy Peas as one of their standard side dishes, much as French Fries are listed at McDonald's.

As we traveled south, there were signs for St. David's, Wales, the smallest city in the United Kingdom and the resting place of Saint David, the patron saint of Wales. We were excited to visit St. David's Cathedral. The cathedral, built in the 12th century, is still in use for Anglican services, and it was one of the most important shrines of medieval Christianity. David was the founder of a strict monastic order, and pilgrimages to St. David's were a very important part of medieval religious life.

We would be in St. David's for a week at our RCI Timeshare exchange. We had booked a one bedroom condo with full kitchen, bathroom, parlor, and all the amenities. St. David's Vacation Club was the name of the timeshare. Located right in the middle of the little city, we could walk to the local market, to the cathedral, and to many parks and lovely outdoor spots.

Every summer, one of the highlights of St, David's is the Cathedral Festival, an annual celebration of classical music and the Welsh heritage of the male choir. There is also an Eisteddfod, an annual competition for Welsh poets and musicians, especially male choirs, at which prizes are given out for compositions and performances. Usually the town's male choir is made up of locals — shopkeepers, policemen, teachers, industrial workers, farmers, all sorts o folks! The choirs we heard at this festival were no exception. It was so wonderful to see townsfolk coming together for the love of music.

The Eisteddfod we attended was spectacular. Imagine an ancient stone cathedral filled with six male choirs who sing in exquisite four-part harmony with superb diction and tonal perfection. The sound transported me to another world. And then, when all of the choirs sang together, the sound was unbelievable. That experience was enough to have made the entire trip worthwhile.

Our week at St. David's was not without its humor. Although we still had our rental car, it remained parked in the car park most of the week. We found that walking through the tiny city was the best way to really become acquainted with local culture and customs. We frequented the local market and bought the stuff of our breakfasts and lunches and dinners. Translating English/Welsh pounds and shillings into the American dollar was a bit challenging, but shopkeepers were very willing to help.

We also bought some laundry detergent as our unit had a washer/dryer and it was high time for some clean clothes. We figured out the washing machine instructions and the dryer as well. But it wasn't until we had done four loads of wash that we realized that the dryer air was not vented to the outdoors but just recirculated back into the apartment unit. Everything kept getting damper and damper, and it was not just because we had some rainy weather.

As our week at St. David's drew to a close, we were packing up in preparation for the journey back to the states.

We drove to Cardiff, returned the rental car, and took the train back to London, where it was one more hotel night and the hotel van to Heathrow Airport.

Rolling Backwards

I rolled backwards and heard someone warn,
"Hey, watch where you're going!"
as if I had eyes in the back of my head.
Well, you never know.
I considered the possibilities.
Maybe I could grow new eyes that would peek
from behind blonde-brown strands,
hair that had never been colored,
always freshly coiffed.
Making a five-point turn,
I found a new view,
different belt buckles, different waistlines.
Glasses dripped drops of Merlot;
Cracker crumbs fell on my arm.
Above my head conversations flourished.
Undertones of last night's dinner party,
the vacation of a lifetime,
the importance of having a retirement plan.
"Whose voice is that?" I wondered to myself,
as somewhere in the stratosphere,
someone said, "And I just had the door jambs refinished."
"What about living in a tent?" I mused.
Wide doorways, expansive walls, room for all.
I rolled backwards again,
bumping into experience,
saluting the spirit of my life.

Selected for publication in "Bone & Tissue,"
Inglis House Poetry Workshop Chapbook, September, 2009

The Flag of Sweden: Yellow on Blue

Chapter Three
Heritage Jamestown
My immigrant family – Half Swedish (my maternal line)

Family stories through the years have been added to and embellished through conversations with my late parents, aunts and uncles, and cousins. The tales have also been expanded through remembrances from my siblings and through Ancestry.com.

In 1944 we moved from Freeport to Jamestown, New York and lived with my mother's parents in a frame house on Bowen Street. When she was six years old, Grandmother Matilda Gustava Johnson, born in Sweden November 28, 1874, had come to America with her parents and siblings. My maternal grandfather was John Henry Hultgren, born in Vadstena, Sweden, May 22, 1875. He had come to America with his parents and siblings, Nov. 1, 1880. They settled in Jamestown, where there was a large Swedish immigrant community.

My Swedish forebears came from places named Narshult and Lemmhut and and Korsberga and other small villages. My great grandparents came to the United States with their five children and celebrated their 62nd anniversary in 1926. Their children died of illnesses like typhoid and diphtheria that are now unheard of as causes of death in the US.

I remember to this day the great shock of white hair that my Swedish grandfather, Grandpa Henry Hultgren, had to the day he died. The house on Bowen Street housed my mother's family on the first floor and another family, the Carlsons, on the second floor. The daguerreotypes that survive of my Swedish ancestors show the men in three piece suits, with stiff collars, and the women in starched white blouses and long wool skirts, with long hair swept up in severe buns. I so wished that my mother and her relatives had labeled the pictures with names. But unfortunately, that information is lost to history. They were a devout Lutheran family whose voices filled the church choir. My grandfather sang tenor solos. Grandpa Henry worked in a furniture factory in Jamestown.

On the following page is a poem I wrote as a remembrance of my grandfather and the legacy of the work he did in that factory.

My Grandfather Had Mahogany Fingers

My grandfather had mahogany fingers
From staining tables in the furniture factory.
Red in his skin,
Maroon under his nails.
It was permanent.
My Swedish grandfather,
Born in Goteborg,
 one of the huddled masses,
 one of the tempest tossed.
His shock of thick white hair stayed with him
 to the grave.
That is how I remember him,
With white hair and mahogany fingers,
As he jounced me on his foot
As he sang
 "Rheea Rheea Rhunka.
 Hadsta nea blunka,
 Vord Stata Nea"
That childhood rhyme that had no translation,
And the white hair,
And the mahogany fingers,
That had no other syntax.

First Place — The Portrait Poem Award —
South Dakota State Poetry Society, 2011

My Grandmother Hultgren died before I was old enough to remember her. But I do recall that we lived in the Bowen Street house for a while around 1945 to 1947 as my father was trying to find permanent employment. I went to kindergarten in Jamestown, walking to school with Christine Carlson from downstairs and with Barbara Fried from across the street. I still have one Brownie Kodak print of the three of us. We are wearing hand me downs from somewhere, and Christine and I have barrettes in our hair and big safety pins holding our coats closed at the neck. Barbara has long brown braids that are looped up from the back of the head over each ear. She was about nine and Christine and I are about five.

My sister Linda was born in Jamestown in 1947 during a huge snowstorm. My father told stories about how he had to shovel the driveway to get the car out to take my mother to the hospital. It was February, and Jamestown is in that area of New York known as the snow belt, with winds whipping off Lake Erie and piling up to three or four feet of snow at a time. So my sister arrived in a snowstorm, and I had a baby sister. I was thrilled.

The Bowen street kitchen always smelled of flour and baking. Spritz butter cookies and Danish pastries filled my senses with delight. Perhaps that is where I got my love for baking—one of those activities that has since become one of my losses. My mother was born in Jamestown, July 23, 1909. She had two sisters. Her oldest sister was Beatrice Lilly Marie (Feb. 14, 1899 – 1970). Beatrice died in her 80s at Gowanda State Hospital, having had schizophrenia all her life. I remember my mother sending her practical gifts at Christmas time—flannel nightgowns and sweaters. She never told me anything about her sister except that she could play the piano and had very long hair, down past her waist. Her other sister was Mildred Ruby Caroline (July 17, 1901 – Dec. 19, 1910), who died of pleurisy.

My mother also had one brother, my Uncle Harold (Nov. 29, 1903 – 1974). He and his wife, Ann, lived with their big cat in a duplex a few blocks from my grandparents. Uncle Harold was a chain smoker and so thin that his ribs showed through his shirt. He worked as a department store manager. Aunt Ann used to knit Christmas sweaters for my sister Linda and me. They were always sent on time, but they were always so small they felt like sausage casings when we put them on. Aunt Ann and Uncle Harold never had any kids, and we only saw then occasionally, so my guess is that Aunt Ann had no idea what size clothing my sister and I wore.

My mother always made us put on the sweaters and have our pictures taken so we could send thank you notes to Aunt Ann. I figured it was my duty. And even now, when I send cards and gifts to my great nieces and great nephews and do not receive a thank you note or any acknowledgement that the gift was even received, I am a bit perturbed and think how times have changed. Hardly anyone sends written notes any more. Now, I would be thrilled with a text or an email!

The Flag of Italy:
Green, White and Red

Chapter Four
Heritage Phillipsburg, New Jersey
The Paternal Half of my Immigrant Family — the Italians

My father's Italian side of the family was large and fleshy and loud. I had three aunts with spouses as uncles, lots of cousins, plus assorted other relations who I knew existed but never met. One story told of the ravioli factory they presumably owned in Jersey City. When we visited in Phillipsburg, New Jersey, we stayed at my *Nonna's* (grandmother in Italian) house on Heckman Street. *Nonno* (grandfather) had passed away before I was born so I never got to meet the man who had started raising grapes in the back yard or who had come to America with his skills as a silk weaver.

My paternal grandfather, Dominic Vago, was born Dec. 8, 1868 in Italy, near Lake Como, and emigrated to the US on board the ship *the Spree* that departed from Genoa, Italy, March 7, 1894; when he was 26 years old. My paternal grandmother was named Angelina Berresone (Berasconi). She married Dominic and they settled in Phillipsburg, New Jersey, and had five children. One boy, Joseph, died after he was kicked by a horse. Ida Vago married Abraham Taiana and had one child. Ines Vago married Henry Thyhsen and had two children. Anita Vago married James Taylor and had 3 children, and my father, Frank Vago, married Florence Hultgren and had four children.

Early on in their marriage, my Italian grandparents had made their home into a boarding house where Italian men could live until they had earned enough money to send for their wives and families to come join them in America. My Nonna kept up the boarding house even after Nonno passed away. The men who lived there loved the authentic Italian food they were provided and the opportunity to continue to speak their native language.

My Aunt Ida and her husband Uncle Abe lived in a sturdy brick bungalow right at the back of Nonna's property. There was a path leading from Nonna's back door along the side wall of the house, across a bit of the yard, and through the gate to Aunt Ida's house. There was a small covered porch at Aunt Ida's back door and we used to sit there and shell peas and pass the time of day. I always wished I'd had the chance to learn Italian but at that time, the rule was that you had to learn English so you could assimilate. Nevertheless, my Nonna and all of her children and their spouses spoke Italian to each other. My father was fluent in Italian, but I could never get him to teach me the language.

When I was about seven, several Saturdays a year, my father and mother loaded my sister Linda and me into the family car — a 1946 Ford — and we drove from Long Island, across the Brooklyn Bridge, across Manhattan, through the Holland Tunnel to New Jersey, along the Pulaski Skyway to Route 22, and on to Phillipsburg to visit my Nonna and all the Italian relatives. My sister, being five years younger, was always asking, "Are we there yet?"

I recognized many of the landmarks along the way, from the mustard-colored tiles inside the Holland Tunnel to the tall teepee along Route 22, where we usually made a bathroom stop before we were "almost there." I was big enough to see out the open windows in the back seat and could recognize when we left the soot and grime of Jersey City and got to the green beginnings of the rolling hills of then-rural New Jersey.

I knew when we got there we would be greeted by Nonna on her front porch. She would have her graying black hair swept back with tortoise shell combs. She always wore black cotton stockings and sturdy black tie shoes with thick Cuban heels. And always an apron of colorful print calico, with wide straps and a big pocket edged with rick rack.

As soon as the car was parked in front of the house, my sister and I raced up to the porch to be enveloped in Nonna's big hug. Nothing about her was timid or small. She always smelled like garlic and tomatoes and Ivory soap. And she always stood back, looked us right in the eye, pinched our cheeks, and said, "What? They don't feed you?" And she would laugh a big belly laugh.

Nonna's house had two sets of stairs; the back stairs went from the attic right down three flights into the kitchen. My sister and I could hear the grown-ups talking in Italian and translating to English for my mother. And I could smell the sauce and feel the excitement and sense all the gestures.

Then Nonna told my sister and me to run up to the attic where we would find two army cots made up for us with fresh sheets that had been dried on the clothesline so they smelled like fresh cut grass. Quilts and pillows completed the welcoming attic scene.

The attic was a magical place because it had plain, unfinished wooden floors and two windows that went all the way down to the floor. We could sit on the floor and see everything that happened on Heckman Street. As I remember, the house across the street was very large, and had a black wrought iron fence all around it. The lawns were expansive and well groomed. The two large statues of deer that flanked the driveway were so life-like that my sister and I were sure they were real. We asked Nonna if we could go across the street and feed the deer. She said they were statues, and we were not allowed to go over there because the rich people lived there and we were not rich. I think that was the first time I came face to face with the idea of rich and not rich. We always had enough to eat and a cozy home to live in. It would take some time for this new idea to be understood.

My Uncle Abe had intimated something similar when he told stories about being an Italian immigrant. My favorite story was the tale of when he was about six and was sent down the street to get a pail of beer for his father. Along the way he had been called names that he did not understand. When he got back with the beer, he asked his father, "What that mean 'Dago'?"

His father said, "You find out. You find out!"

Trapunto

In my grandmother's face,
Stitched into the hexagons and pinwheels
Of longing and remembering.
I see the gathers of children, the pleats of time,
Spanning the years like *entredeux* between body and spirit.
I trace her face from forehead to chin,
Feeling the embroidery of births and losses,
A face made into wearable art
            by goodbyes, by joys, by deaths.
Artificial masks are surrendered.
Winter's freezes and summer's thaws
Have created a countenance that recorded
Life's many years connected by touch, look, word.
The patchwork of a life,
Pintucks of brow and cheek set into an album quilt,
The *trapunto* of generations.

Second Honorable Mention - Connections Award -

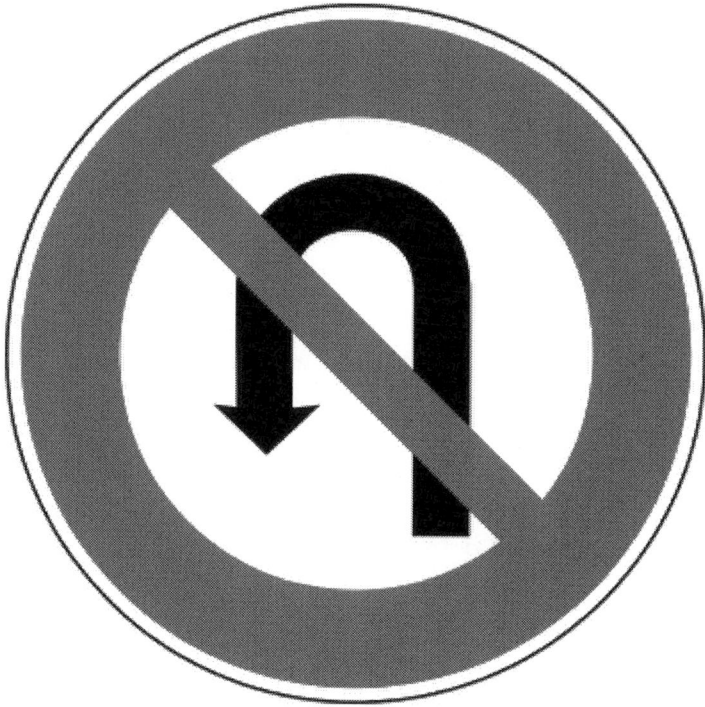

No U Turn

"Jesus wants me for a Sunbeam"

Learned in Sunday School in the undercroft of the Episcopal Church of the Transfiguration, Freeport, New York.

Jesus wants me for a sunbeam
To shine for him each day;
In ev'ry way try to please him,
At home, at school, at play.

[Chorus]
A sunbeam, a sunbeam,
Jesus wants me for a sunbeam.
A sunbeam, a sunbeam,
I'll be a sunbeam for him.

Jesus wants me to be loving
And kind to all I see,
Showing how pleasant and happy
His little one can be.
Chorus

Words: Nellie Talbot
Music: Edwin O. Excell, 1851–1921

Chapter Five
Freeport, the Rectory, the Beginning

Who could have imagined when I was born that the music of the Episcopal Church would be the musical score that would wind through my life and follow and support me through more than 70 years. From *Jesus Wants me for a Sunbeam*, that nursery song I learned in the undercroft of the Church of the Transfiguration to the *The Strife is O'er*, that Palestrina hymn that celebrates resurrection that I have chosen for my eventual Memorial Service.

I am what many call a "cradle Episcopalian." My cradle in 1942, was housed in the rectory of the Episcopal Church of the Transfiguration in Freeport, New York, a church completed in July 1894, where even today, the Baptismal Font and tapestry are the same ones that were there in 1942 when I was baptized by the Reverend Dr. Reginald Heber Scott, Transfiguration's longest serving rector. Do you think that the magnetism of the church was so strong even then that I have retained my appreciation of stained glass and carved wooden Reredos such as were in the Church where I was baptized? My love of the Anglican tradition, the language of the Book of Common Prayer, the music of the church, and the concept of the three-legged stool to represent the foundation of the Episcopal Church in Scripture, tradition, and reason, were undoubtedly begun and nurtured from my days in the cradle at the Episcopal Church of the Transfiguration.

I was born at the LeRoy Sanitarium in New York City where my mother was a nurse. The LeRoy Sanitarium was a place where actors and the wealthy went for a "respite" and "rehab." My mother, Florence, took care of some famous people. I remember seeing a photo of movie star Henry Fonda addressed "to Flossie with gratitude." She was present for the delivery of the Fonda children, Jane and Peter. Primarily a private treatment facility for wealthy people, the LeRoy was also a maternity hospital. Aristotle Onassis' daughter Christina was born there in 1950. Celebrities Nat King Cole and Judy Garland were treated there. The hospital closed in 1980.

My mother and her best friend Virginia, both nurses, lived together for a time in New York. Through Virginia, my mother met my dad Frank who was searching for work during the last years of the Great Depression. He could not find satisfactory employment, although he had taken a number of correspondence classes and had worked for Macy's selling furniture. Eventually he found employment with Con Ed and then in 1948 was hired by American Electric Power to design electrical substations. When Frank and Florence married, Virginia and her husband Clif got housing for them in the unoccupied Rectory of the Episcopal Church of the Transfiguration, where Clif was head of the Church Vestry. That is where they were living when I, a war baby, was born. Virginia became my godmother and Clif, my godfather. They became Aunt Virginia and Uncle Clif.

My mother received her nurses' training at the Sisters of Charity Hospital in Buffalo, New York. When she graduated, the tradition of the Capping Ceremony was a standard of commencement. Nurses were presented with their starched white caps to signify their acceptance into the long line of nurses that began with Florence Nightingale, who pledged to care for the sick. Now considered old-fashioned, the uniform of the nurse, a starched white knee-length dress and the white cap, white stockings and white shoes, presented a clean and professional picture of one of the most honored careers for women in the early 20th century.

I recall how my mother took pride in her nursing uniform and how proud she was of her career, devoting most of her life to that profession. I did not follow my mother's career choice, although my younger sister Linda did, as did my older sister Carolyn. The need to care for people was very evident in my mother and my sisters. They always went out of their way to lend a hand, to help tend the sick, to be concerned for other people. I think that is a quality that has stuck with me, although not in a medical way, but rather in my role as a teacher and counselor and advocate for people with disabilities. We each find the path that suits our abilities and our training. I am thankful that I had good support from my family in my search for a meaningful career.

There are so many family stories about wonderful visits at Aunt Virginia's house in Freeport. There was a huge kitchen with stools all around the counter. We would all sit at the counter and have snacks and meals. This is where I first tasted beef tongue. It was very much like ham. Back then, it seems every part of the animal was cooked and eaten. World War II shortages caused rationing which began in 1941 when President Roosevelt created the Office of Price Administration, which set price controls and consumption limits through rationing. The first ration cards were issued in May of 1942, just a few months before I was born. The first card was known as the "Sugar Card" for one of the items that could be purchased with that particular ration card. Other cards were issued as the war went on and commodities became scarcer and scarcer. Things like gasoline, tires, fuel oil, nylon, shoes, along with household staples like meat, dairy, coffee, jams, lard, shortening, and flour were rationed. Rationing sacrifices were looked on as one's patriotic duty. It was the norm. Even today in 2021, my husband and I recall our parents re-using a square of waxed paper and call things like that our "world war II mentality." Nothing went to waste.

My parents had a Victory Garden on the grounds of the rectory. Everyone had a Victory Garden so they could raise fresh vegetables as a sacrificial contribution to the war effort. On the rectory grounds there was also a huge black walnut tree that yielded walnuts that were used in family desserts and treats. There were also lots of squirrels that loved living in that tree, scampering around and shaking the nuts down to the ground. The squirrels also could leap from the tree to the roof of the house and wiggle their way into the attic. There were many family stories of hearing the squirrels scampering up in the attic rafters.

One family story recounts how on one late fall day in 1942, my sister Carolyn, who was then 15, was tending to me in my rolling bassinet on the grounds of the rectory. A squirrel baby had been dislodged from its nest and had fallen into my bassinet. The mother squirrel leaped down from the tree to rescue her baby, and Carolyn tried to shoo it away. The mother squirrel bit my sister as she grabbed her squirrel-baby and scurried away back up the tree. My sister had to go to the doctor to have stitches and anti-rabies vaccine. But I am forever grateful for her saving me from the mama squirrel.

I recall many other storied events that took place in Freeport, especially at Aunt Virginia's house. She was quite the seamstress, as was my mother. She had a daughter named Elizabeth, nicknamed Betsy, who became like a cousin to me. Betsy was just one year older than I was so our relationship was very close. Our two brothers, Richard (Dick) my brother and Clif Jr. (Tommy) Betsy's brother, also became good friends. When Betsy and I were about three and four, we were left at Aunt Virginia's house being "baby sat" by our brothers, who were then about twelve and fourteen. The story goes that the boys were occupied playing Chinese Checkers and Betsy and I were left to occupy ourselves. Well, you can figure something would happen. Betsy wanted to play "Beauty Parlor." She found a towel in the bathroom that she put around my shoulders as I sat on an ottoman in the living room. She found a pair of Aunt Virginia's sewing shears and began to cut my hair just like at the Beauty Parlor.

I had long "baloney curls" that were just right for a four-year-old to grasp and chop off. And chop she did. We thought it was great fun. We were being so grown up. When Betsy was done, I had the equivalent of a buzz cut with hairs sticking out all over my head in no particular order. All my long curls were scattered on the floor like so many doggie tails. The story goes that my mother came back with Aunt Virginia and screamed bloody hell at the sight of me with very little hair. The two boys were in deep trouble. My mother phoned the salon at Best & Company in Garden City and with the voice of a desperate mother pleaded with the operator to see if she could bring me right in to the salon. Betsy was scolded for using her mother's sewing shears. My mother was in tears for the rest of the day.

Chapter Six
Farmingdale

My father bought the house at 22 Pinehurst Road in Farmingdale, Long Island, New York, in 1948 because he could walk in 10 minutes to the Long Island Rail Road train station and commute into the job he got as an electrical substation designer in New York City.

Number 22 was a typical suburban ticky-tacky house like those that had popped up all over Long Island after World War II: Two bedrooms, one bath, kitchen, living room, basement, and unfinished attic. My father laid floorboards in the unfinished attic space so my brother could have the semblance of a bedroom. My older sister stayed in Phillipsburg for a couple of years and then went away to Nursing School in Philadelphia. My mom and dad moved my one-year-old sister, five-year-old me, and my brother in the spring of 1948 from Jamestown into the new house in Farmingdale with its paved street and sidewalk, a yard covered with sand and gravel, one tree, five front steps commonly called the "stoop," and five steps at the back door just called the "back steps." Nothing like the 2,500 square foot "open concept designs" of the HGTV houses of the 21st century, our cozy home still did okay for us.

My sister Linda and I shared the back bedroom and, as the calendar pages turned, we stuffed our lives into two twin beds, one four-foot-wide closet, two dressers, a small bookcase, a small desk, and two desk chairs. We made tents out of bedding, trains out of the chairs, and created a sisterly relationship that has withstood more than seventy years of good and bad times. Sitting on the back steps we would massage packages of white margarine with its imbedded orange disc until the whole package turned yellow and resembled butter. We got our first dog, Archie, and used a big iron container as a bathtub to fill with water from the hose in the back yard so we could give him a bath. We received skates for birthdays and clamped them on to our shoes and skated with neighbor kids on the neighborhood sidewalks to see who could go fastest without falling and scraping knees. Getting two-wheel bikes was an amazing milestone that was marked by new rules of behavior. The streets and sidewalks of our neighborhood were perfect for bike riding and roller skating.

A typical Farmingdale home of the post World War II era.

Everyone knew everyone else and contact with parents was just a phone call or a quick walk away. You couldn't get away with anything! One Saturday, I sat with my sister on our front stoop and told her to go across the street and tell Kerry Reynolds (name changed) that nobody liked her. My sister did that, and within five minutes Kerry's father was at our door talking to my dad. Apologies were instantly forthcoming.

With other kids in the neighborhood, I rode my bike round and round the block and thought I was pretty hot

The back of our simple home in Farmingdale, New York.

stuff and could ride very fast with no problems. My bragging and racing soon came to an end with a fall, and skinned knees imbedded with gravel and dirt. My mother poured hydrogen peroxide over the scrape until the bubbling stopped. Then she used tweezers to pick out the gravel, rocks, debris, and dirt. She washed the wound with soap and water and then applied iodine, a gauze bandage and tape. I had a scar on my knee for nearly twenty years.

Now, in 2021, I cannot mount a stationary bike or even a recumbent bike just to get a modicum of needed exercise. Gone are the days of freewheeling on my 26-inch turquoise blue, secondhand bike, feeling the wind ruffle through my hair as I whirled around the neighborhood with not a care in the world. Those were the days of attaching playing cards to the spokes of my bike wheels so the clickety clack, clickety clack could create a rhythm and keep time with the band at the Fourth of July parade.

The camaraderie of the neighborhood bike . . .

"Hey. Jill! Can you come out and ride?"

"Barbara, do you have to practice or can you come out for a bike race?"

"Hi, Pam. Your new bike looks great with those streamers coming out of the handlebar grips!"

There was always someone to hang out with, someone to share fun and adventure with. There was always someone to be a friend.

But now, since the 1990s, my life as a wheelchair user has become a life of quiet interior reflection. I have become my own friend, my own entertainer, my own event planner. The Jill and Barbara and Pam of my childhood neighborhood have all moved away. They took their bikes and roller skates and found new neighborhoods. I too have found a new neighborhood, but it is one very different from the one I knew in my childhood. Those are just memories now, in my current days of wheelchair seating, reading, and dreaming.

Because I was not a sports-minded kid, my entrance into the community of people with disabilities was probably easier than it would have been had I been a tennis or field hockey superstar. I did not have to hang up my uniform or my Nikes nor give up a resume of honors and accolades for physical activities or sports. I did not have a collection of sports trophies or videos of my prowess at basketball or volleyball. Rather I had a collection of stellar report cards and lists of books that I had read and assimilated. My curriculum vitae is sedentary and bookish. A disability that put me in a wheelchair, at a desk, at a podium with a moveable microphone, or at a kitchen table with a peer with a disability, would give me a chance for success.

My childhood was primarily academic, musical, artistic, and language-based, filled with books and conversations, ballet lessons, piano lessons, chorus, sewing and crafts, simple neighborhood games. I was not good at sports; in elementary school, I was the last one chosen for kick ball and relay races. In high school, I was the flag bearer for the annual Sports Night so I did not have to play basketball or display my lack of adeptness at gymnastics. But I was asked to be on the debate team and on the student judicial council. I was a Girl Scout for several years and earned badges in cooking and in crafts, and ultimately, in horsemanship,

Perhaps my only foray into a sport was as a Girl Scout when I took horseback riding lessons at the Bethpage State Park Stables and learned to ride the polo ponies that were stabled there. The spring and summer of 1955, our Girl Scout troop was chosen to form the Girl Scout Equestrian Drill Team and to perform at the Nassau County Fair. For my non-athletic self to actually be chosen for an athletic event was absolutely overwhelming. Our leader choreographed our moves and worked out the many patterns and maneuvers that we had to learn and practice before the big show. We walked and trotted and cantered in lines and circles. Timing, coordination, alignment, horsemanship, all were under scrutiny as we performed. We all wore tan jodhpurs, riding boots, helmets, and our green Girl Scout jackets. Our team performed well and was written up in the local Long Island newspaper, *Newsday*, describing the precise lines and complex routines, coordinated rotations, measured pacing, turns and pivots, with drills executed with barely perceptible signals from riders to horses. The polo ponies from Bethpage State Park were ideal mounts for our drill team as the ponies were trained to follow the slightest signals from their riders through leg pressure, small movements of the reins, and the shift of the riders' weight.

My athletic days were short-lived, though, as the Equestrian Drill Team was disbanded after that summer and I was not able to continue riding. I missed the polo ponies; they were stocky and gentle and responded to me with nuzzles and head pokes. I could whisper to them and they lifted up their heads as if to say, "Where have you been? It's time for a little adventure."

Number 22

I will go there once again,
To the white house on the little street,
The ticky-tacky 1948 house
With two bedrooms and one bathroom,
A yard scraped clean of grass and potatoes.
The one with a cement stoop at the front door
And the number 22 in black iron numbers.
22 has had clogged sinks,
Deep cracks in the sidewalk.
This is the house that pulls everyone back,
For pictures that show changing hair styles,
Easter finery from Robert Hall,
Blowing out candles on heavily frosted birthday cakes,
A baby's first Christmas and a grandma's last,
High school graduations and great aunts' funerals.
Through the generations, #22 stayed constant.
The parents died,
But the next generation kept the house
Adding more bedrooms,
Another bathroom, an improved kitchen.
The third generation lives there now,
And many of the fourth come back for extended visits.
To ride their bikes around the block
Just like the second generation did,
To walk to the train station and imagine
Meeting a great grandfather as he came home
From work in the city
To #22.

Judith Krum (2020)

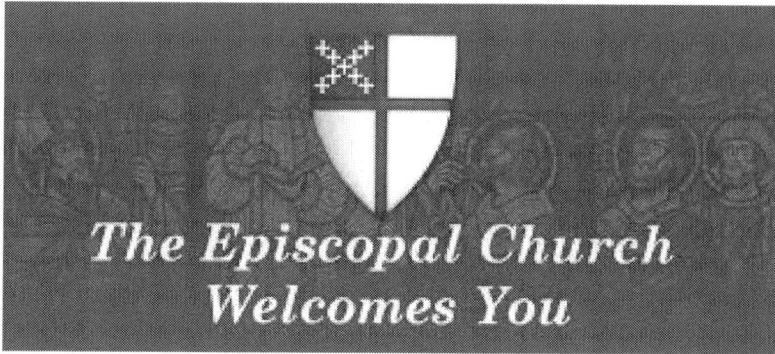

The Episcopal Church Welcomes You

Chapter Seven
St. Thomas Episcopal Church, Farmingdale, New York

*The music of the church gets louder and the green
suede notebook becomes a mantra*

Though I was a cradle Episcopalian, it wasn't until the early 1950s when I was at St. Thomas Episcopal Church in Farmingdale, Long Island, New York, that I became fully immersed in the life of the church. I finally was old enough to understand the church's teachings and the sacraments. From 1950 when I was in elementary school in Farmingdale to 1960 when I graduated from high school and went off to Marietta College in Marietta, Ohio, St. Thomas was part of my daily and weekly life. Sunday School, choir, preparation for Confirmation and Confirmation itself on December 22, 1955, and helping in the church nursery, all were part of my day to day activities. I also attended the Diocesan summer camp, Camp De Wolfe in Wading River, Long Island, and became acquainted with the sisters of St. John the Baptist through a Retreat at their Mother House.

St. Thomas was my refuge as I grew to appreciate the language of the church in the *Book of Common Prayer (BCP)*.

At that time it was the 1928 *BCP* with its *thee's* and *thou's* and wondrous use of Elizabethan language. Since then the "new" 1979 *BCP* has been adopted with its more inclusive and modern language. Singing in the choir from the back balcony of the church was one of my most memorable experiences. The choir director was a summer employee of the Good Humor Ice Cream Company, and he used to wear his Good Humor shirts with their white epaulets on the shoulders. He was also the director of the school chorus.

And it was at St. Thomas where I had my first encounter with advocacy and, when remembering my Uncle Abe's story of being called names because he was an Italian, what would become my passion for justice. The priest at St. Thomas from 1950 to 1966 was Father Hampshire, a larger than life man with a passion for education and fair play. I learned the Prayer of Baptism by heart under his tutelage. But as times have changed, so has the language of the *BCP*, although the message and the sacraments have remained steadfast. The *BCP* prayers and references from here on are quoted from the 1979 *BCP* because the current language more fully reflects my thoughts.

Let us pray.

Heavenly Father, we thank you that by water and the Holy Spirit you have bestowed upon *these* your servants the forgiveness of sin, and have raised *them* to the new life of grace. Sustain *them,* O Lord, in your Holy Spirit. Give *them* an inquiring and discerning heart, the courage to will and to persevere, a spirit to know and to love you, and the gift of joy and wonder in all your works. *Amen.*

And the question posed at Baptism and again at Confirmation when the Celebrant asks:

"Will you strive for justice and peace among all people, and respect the dignity of every human being?" and the answer: "I will with God's help."

From these words and the role models I found through St. Thomas Church, I developed a deep passion for living into those words. The first strong example came from Father Hampshire himself when I witnessed his preparation for participation in a 1961 Prayer Pilgrimage to protest segregation. Though I was at Marietta College in November of 1961, I was well aware of Father Hampshire's mission. The Pilgrimage was reported in *Jet Magazine*, Vol. XXI, no.3, Nov. 9, 1961, which provided these details:

Father W. Robert Hampshire, for 17 years rector of St. Thomas Episcopal Church in Farmingdale, Long Island, New York, was one of the 28 Episcopal clergymen who, in November of 1961, made a Prayer Pilgrimage from New Orleans to Detroit with 15 arrests along the way, for their mission to cleanse Christ's body of segregation and separation. Father Hampshire said, "A lot of people would rather just ignore segregation and they didn't approve of the Pilgrimage, thought it undignified. Most of the reaction seems to be against the idea of breaking local laws; we must keep the little laws even if they contradict the 'Big Law'." Noting that many of his parishioners had expressed their displeasure by getting out before "I even got to the door'" he added, "I imagine it will pass."

An African American priest, the Rev. C. Robert Chapman, for 10 years pastor in Hempstead, New York, said, "Although not receiving any negative reaction, I didn't get much praise either." The week following the Pilgrimage, he took office as the Executive Secretary of the New York branch of the NAACP. He said that this role reflected his feeling that, "I must complement the pastoral ministry of praying and giving sacraments, with taking action."

Another African American priest, the Rev. Powell Woodward, Vicar of St, George's Church, Chadwick, New York, was one of the 15 clergy arrested at the bus station in Jackson, Mississippi, for seeking to eat together with his clergy colleagues, both black and white.

When I came home from Marietta to Farmingdale for the December 1960-61 Christmas vacation, news of the Pilgrimage was readily discussed. I was so proud to be a member of the congregation where Father Hampshire actually lived the promise "to strive for justice and peace among all people and to respect the dignity of every human being."

At Marietta College, I had joined a sorority that on paper said it was open to pledging girls from racial minorities. Unfortunately, it did not live up to its word .The Marietta Chapter had invited a Black girl to pledge, but when the national organization found out about it, the girl was asked to remove herself from the pledge class. I was outraged. At that point all I could think of was Father Hampshire on his Prayer Pilgrimage and how he lived his faith promises. I wrote a letter to the National Organization saying I was withdrawing from the local chapter because of their lack of racial justice. I received a letter back that said my name was to be stripped from the Green Suede Notebook. I could just imagine some national sorority officer standing on a podium with a huge pair of scissors and holding a large tome called the Green Suede Notebook and cutting my name out of a list of sorority sisters.

From that time on, I was an independent at Marietta and could be friends with whomever I wanted. I developed friendships with several Black students, some Jewish students, and some others that gave me a chance to "strive for justice and peace and to respect the dignity of every human being." To this day the episode of the Green Suede Notebook lives on as my mantra of the fulfilling my Baptismal promise. Other examples over the years have involved advocating for the Americans with Disabilities Act and becoming friends with many from the LGBTQ community.

From then on I have had opportunities to advocate for justice and for human dignity, working with the independent living movement for people with disabilities, for organizations for sexual diversity and inclusion, for women's rights and equal pay, for the rights of pregnant teenagers to continue to attend school, and so many others.

Chapter Eight
Marietta College

The 1960s — Recalculating after the Death of JFK

I was in college during the early 1960s at Marietta College in southern Ohio. There I was shaped by relationships and current events. One of my most memorable activities at Marietta was being Editor of the college's weekly student newspaper, the Marcolian. The position came with responsibilities and opportunities. Column inches were filled and editorials were written. Headlines were composed and deep friendships were developed. It was a time before cell phones and the internet. We relied on television and radio news and messages that came in over the teletype machines from various national news sources. Our main focus was the reporting of campus news and reactions of students to national and state events.

But that focus was changed drastically in 1963. Several Marcolian staff members and I drove to Southern Illinois University in Carbondale, Illinois, for a two-day, November 22-23, Journalism conference for Midwestern college newspaper staffs. We had driven most of the night to arrive at the university by noon on November 22. All sorts of workshops were offered, led by professional newspaper people from all over the Midwest and the East. After registering, we took a few moments to check in to our rooms and freshen up. At that point we had TV news on display in our respective hotel rooms. And there it was. Walter Cronkite, announcing with cracking voice and tear-stained face, that shortly after noon on November 22, 1963, President John F. Kennedy was assassinated as he rode in a motorcade through Dallas, Texas.

I still get a pit in my stomach thinking about that day and that time. I joined my college friends and we hugged and cried in disbelief. The Journalism Conference was cancelled since all of the speakers and workshop leaders had to leave to go back to their respective publications in order to cover this horrific event. The Southern Illinois College campus was suddenly deserted and eerily quiet. We were all so devastated by the news. There was nothing to do except to drive back to Marietta. As I recall, we didn't speak but a few words during that journey of more than 500 miles. We listened to the news reports on the radio and silently wept for our loss and for the country's loss. There were no cell phones, no Facebook, no twitter. There was just AM or FM radio.

On the following two pages are copies of articles published in the Marietta College newspaper, *the Marcolian*, reporting on student reaction on campus to the assassination of President Kennedy in 1963. The author was editor of the paper.

With the assassination of President John F. Kennedy on November 22, 1963, the lives of Americans everywhere, including those of students attending classes at Marietta College, were suddenly and shockingly disrupted. A few weeks later, on Friday, December 13, *The Marcolian* carried a two-page feature commemorating the day that would never be forgotten. Students' reactions to the loss of the nation's leader were poignantly described by *Marcolian* editor Judith Vago, Class of 1964:

By two o'clock we all knew and our knowledge was marked by silence and furrowed brows. At twenty to three as Erwin's bells chimed the finality of the day, professors quietly closed their books and dismissed class. Most students went directly to the Student Center, many walking alone, others in twos and threes. In the Center there was no rock and roll blaring from the juke box. There was only the measured voice of Walter Cronkite telling us the President of the United States was dead. We had many thoughts, many questions, but they were left unanswered as we listened in incredulous silence.

We didn't call him President Kennedy; he was JFK. He was too young. We felt he understood youth, us. We felt he respected us, our beliefs, our problems. We are Baptists, Italians, Lutherans, Catholics, Poles, Jews, Negroes, Irish, Japanese, but we had two things in common at exactly the same time - our youth and our feeling of loss at the death of JFK.

Many things told of this loss. The flag flew at half mast. Students gathered around the campus bulletin board and read teletype releases with the latest news. We read newspapers and found in all of them that the story was true; the President was dead. So we held our heads in our hands for a brief moment to try and believe in the enormity and solemnity of the history we were experiencing.

The Reverend William Smith, assistant professor of religion and philosophy, led the memorial service on Saturday. We wore solemn faces, the rain pattering on our umbrellas as we half-listened, half-thought. Dr. Frank E. Duddy Jr. sent a telegram of condolence which was later acknowledged by President Lyndon B. Johnson.

My MS Journey

Although we cannot see the private moments of grief and bewilderment each of us felt as America buried its President, the experiences we did witness belong to all of us as did JFK himself. He was a twentieth century man with twentieth century ideas. He worked to bring together the cultural, the intellectual, the political. We respected him as a man and a leader.

So it is to the memory of the man we had to give up to the ages that we dedicate this small and insignificant reminder of the fact that 'Now the time has come for this nation to fulfill its promise.' And the youthful walls of freedom echo 'Let us begin.'"

-J. M. V.

We got back to Marietta and found the campus devastated by the news. President John F. Kennedy was dead. As the editor of *The Marcolian*, I recall that day and the following days all too well. Most of the student body was in the Student Center where television monitors had been installed so students could follow the news. I have never seen such a somber group of college students.

At that point, I turned to my job as editor to begin to record the events going on within the college community. I wrote a two-page spread for the college paper that would be published after the Thanksgiving holiday break. Our *Marcolian* photographers took pictures of the sadness and the utter despair they saw among the students. The spread in the *Marcolian* included several of their photographs along with my editor's article. I recall the flag at half mast, the bells in the tower of Erwin Hall tolling their sadness, the memorial service led by the Rev. William Smith, assistant professor of religion and philosophy, as he tried to help us make sense of the killing of the President.

It was raining that day, bringing to mind the final rainy, umbrella-filled scene of Thornton Wilder's play *Our Town* and the character Emily's words after she had lost her life in childbirth, exploring the circle of life and questioning the meaning of life, love, and death. At the end, the recently deceased Emily is granted the chance to revisit one day in her life, and she discovers that she never appreciated all she possessed until she lost it. "Oh, earth, you're too wonderful for anybody to realize you," she says as she takes her place among the dead. And so it was.

Chapter Nine
Bethlehem & Kent & Westminster

Besides major current event happenings, there are other little things that stick with you throughout your life. Upholstery on couches is one of those things. I can still feel that God-awful beige and green, scratchy upholstery on the Sears futon in our living room/bedroom/ study as I started out as a woman with a first job and a first husband living in a two-room $50 a month apartment.

LeRoy and I had married right after college graduation in June 1964, each with a BA in English. We thought we had a great deal in common. We had both read classic British literature, Shakespeare, 19th century prose writers, Irish poetry, American novels and poetry. We had worked together on the college newspaper and the creative writing magazine. He got an assistantship at Lehigh University in Bethlehem, Pennsylvania, to study for his Masters, and I got a position as a speech correctionist (now a speech and language therapist) for the elementary schools, also in Bethlehem. I earned $4800 that first year, and his stipend brought $100 a month. Our budget of $6,000 was tight, but we each had a car—mine, a turquoise Mustang convertible; his, a gray Volkswagen Beetle. Wedding gifts provided pots and pans, dinnerware, flatware, a few linens and blankets. We had books, two typewriters, a radio. This was 1964. What more could we need?

I became an expert on ways to spend less than a dollar a day on our food expenses. It was 1964 and three cans of tuna cost a buck, and a one-pound box of Creamette macaroni cost 35 cents. So there we had, basically, three meals for $1.35 plus a few pantry items like cheese and milk. Cereal was inexpensive and bread was about 22 cents a loaf. The only thing that was impacting our budget was our smoking. A pack of cigarettes was about 35 cents. And everyone smoked, and everyone drank coffee at $.79 a pound. Starbucks had not yet hit the scene so coffee was usually perked at home. The budget remained fairly stable for us for that year. We carted dirty laundry to the laundromat on the corner. We didn't need fancy clothes or expensive electronics. Just simple day-to-day items. As 1964 merged into 1965 and my husband was finishing his Master's Degree, we began to look ahead to the next chapter in the book of life. Besides, the scratchy futon upholstery was wearing very thin.

With his MA in hand, my husband set out to find a PhD program where he could earn his doctorate in English as well as obtain an assistantship that would give us some money to live on, as I applied for teaching positions in public schools. Our searches landed us in Kent, Ohio, where Kent State University offered an excellent PhD program and where the public schools were advertising for English teachers for junior and senior high school classes. The position I got was teaching eighth and ninth grade English at Davey Junior High School. We would be able to make it.

Financially it was a step up from our Bethlehem budget so we could afford a modern one bedroom apartment right in Kent. There was even a laundry room in the basement of our building.

Life was filled with books and teaching. We began to make friends with colleagues and professors, students, and administrators. The scratchy futon was replaced by a real couch upholstered in cranberry nylon frieze from a local discount store. We got an actual double bed frame from a used furniture store and a mattress new from the local Sears. A table and chairs for the kitchen and some brick and board bookcases filled the bill for little cost. We had moved our belongings from Pennsylvania to Ohio in our two cars, both crammed to the limit. We left the futon behind in Bethlehem.

We were in Kent for three years until LeRoy completed his PhD, dissertation and all, in 1968. The next step was a move to Westminster, Maryland, where he got a position as Assistant Professor of English at a small private college, and I secured a job teaching English at North Carroll High School in Manchester, Maryland, about a 20 minute drive north of Westminster. We really started to put down roots in Westminster. We became active in Vietnam War protests, and I, with my passion or justice, learned about civil disobedience and peace and justice, diversity, and inclusiveness. I loved my teaching job and my colleagues at North Carroll.

The English Department at the college was wonderful. They took us under their collective wings and became a kind of family. One couple, Nancy and Del, was particularly helpful as we tried to get settled into our new routine. Their two girls, fraternal twins, were lovely. I gave them my collection of international dolls that I had received from aunts and uncles and grandparents over the years. I guess I wanted to share some of my heritage with a family, like I hoped to have one day.

We bought a house in Westminster, with three bedrooms, two bathrooms, living room, dining room, laundry room, carport, and a basement. We began to entertain colleagues from the college and from my school. We really had friends. I also started thinking about taking classes again so I could earn my Masters in education. Many school systems were then trying to attract teachers with master's degrees. The college in Westminster offered an M.Ed. degree, and as the spouse of a faculty member I could attend for very little cost. Since our marriage in 1964, I had put my own desires for additional education on the back burner in order to support my husband in his quest for higher degrees. But I felt it was my time now. I enrolled in the master's program that would lead to a degree in counseling, so I would qualify for a position as a Guidance Counselor/Guidance Director.

It was a good program, and it felt so good to once again be studying for my own advancement. I participated in counseling practica, research, abnormal psychology, multicultural counseling, various communication techniques, and a culminating research project to study the effects of teenage pregnancy on the graduation rates of school girls. As part of my research project, I interviewed more than 50 pregnant teenage girls in Carroll County, Maryland, to determine if they were planning to complete high school or if there were factors that would preclude their earning their high school diplomas. Although my research took place in 1968/69, I can still recall many of those situations.

Because I desperately wanted to become pregnant myself, getting to know these pregnant teenagers presented emotional stress that I was finding very difficult to deal with. Why were these kids having babies when I—who could offer a loving home and a family just waiting to welcome another niece or nephew or cousin or grandchild— was left empty.

One girl in my research study was living at home with her parents, and she really wanted to finish her senior year. On my first visit to interview her, I was introduced to poverty and living conditions that I found appalling. I could not put my purse or my tote bag on the floor for fear of carrying roaches home with me. After that first meeting, since it was spring time and the weather was nice, I suggested our next meetings take place outside or at the public library. Most of our discussions centered around how she would take care of her baby after it was born and still have time to continue with school. Her parents could not help with the costs of raising a new baby or with daily care of an infant so she could attend school. In the late 1960s there was still a great deal of stigma attached to having a child out of wedlock. Very few day care centers existed for the care of infants, and even so, the costs were prohibitive for her situation. And also, school districts rarely allowed pregnant teenagers, let alone new mothers, to attend schools. There was much work to be done. My master's thesis presented an opportunity to advocate for the teenage mothers as well as to present ideas for systems changes to the school district.

My contacts with all the pregnant teenage girls gave me insights into families and how important children were to these girls. I was feeling left out of the family connections. My husband and I really had everything one could desire. Except children. We had been trying to have kids ever since we moved to Westminster. I had abandoned birth control pills for two years and still no pregnancy. We went to Johns Hopkins Medical Center in Baltimore to get tested to determine what was going on. It was a very difficult time. Counting ovulation days, recording menstrual cycles; sex became a medical procedure instead of an act of love.

We exchanged angry words quite often, and blame bandied back and forth. Nothing was working. Patience had run its course. He took refuge in his college work, college colleagues and students. I took refuge in my work and in community theater. Anything I could do to avoid being myself, that childless woman. Our relationship disintegrated; we separated, and he asked for a divorce because

I could not give him children. Anger does not do justice to my feelings. I had worked hard and supported him as he earned a Master's and PhD. "How dare he?" I screamed inside my head. I came up with a number of epithets and new names for him.

I was so very depressed. All I could do was sink deeper into blaming myself for the collapse of our marriage and the lack of children. Simon and Garfunkel's song "I am a Rock" was my theme song as I prepared to move out of the house in Westminster.

No Ripeness There

He said goodbye.
No sorrow, no regret, no pain, just goodbye.

What happened to commitment?
Throwaway relationships like bald tires sinking in a river.
Years melted into twilight shadows.
Time faded into yellowed newsprint chronicles.
Rehearsed dialogue forgotten on opening night.
Lear's Fool was dead, more sinned upon than sinning.

The pain was searing, red-hot, aching, throbbing.
Broken life, token living.
Forsaken,
Dumped like an empty oil drum,
Thrown away like gnawed-on ribs,
Snake skin left among the rocks,
Abandoned like Anne of Cleves to the Tower of self-doubt.
No ripeness there.

© Judith Krum 2010

I became determined to survive. I had to recalculate. I hired a lawyer and discussed what the next legal steps would be. He kept the house and paid me half of its market value. I kept my turquoise Ford Mustang convertible. I found a new apartment in a town about 10 miles from Westminster and shopped like crazy for new furnishings for it, thanks to the financial settlement on the house. It was the 70s! Everything was flower power and bright colors and I had money to spend. A velvet, lime green sofa, white parson tables for the living room; a white wooden bookshelf; a plush red velvet two-seater swivel chair; a white tulip table and chairs for the dining area of the kitchen. A queen size bed, a triple dresser, and a shelf unit that could be arranged in many ways, with shelves, a desk, and drawer sections.

I still had my sewing machine and so I decided to make curtains for the huge window in the apartment's living room. I found some gorgeous Marimekko sateen fabric with vibrant swaths of green, rose, pink, and orange. I made café curtains for that window, and those curtains have found their way into every home I have had ever since. I believe those fantastic colors helped to lift me from a deep depression into a rainbow of light and hope. Plus, I was showing him that I could survive and actually have a life! I guess there is something called revenge!

Chapter Ten
The 1970s

Recalculating from that low point in my life's journey, my high school students came to my rescue, as many students would again and again. The cast members of the high school production of *A Wizard of Oz* that I had been directing somehow found out where I lived and when the production was over, they all gave me a surprise visit at my apartment, bearing gifts—a pair of rattan chairs with green velvet cushions and a small wooden three-shelf display unit to hang on my wall. How could I despair with students like these looking after me? The Tin Man, the Scarecrow, the Cowardly Lion, Dorothy, Glinda the Good Witch of the South, the Wicked Witch of the West, assorted monkeys and munchkins—we sang "Over the Rainbow" and had cake. The kids had told the bakery to spell the word Wizard with two zz's – Wizzard! It was a marvelous time.

I still have no idea how they got into my apartment, and no one confessed to anything.

There is another thread to the *Wizard of Oz* story. The musical director for the production, the high school's choral director, David, had graduated from the Peabody Conservatory of Music in Baltimore, Maryland. He was dating an English teacher at the school, my friend and colleague JoAnne. It just so happened that David knew a man from Peabody named Randy. And JoAnne, who is really a Yente, decided that she and David would engineer a meeting between Randy and me. David had been Randy's college roommate, so they were very well acquainted.

Over the next few months, bluebirds were flying high and more than17 rainbows appeared. David and JoAnne were married, and Randy was Best Man at their wedding in Pennsylvania. JoAnne was relentless in her efforts to get Randy and me together. She hosted parties at their home where I was invited, as was Randy. Picnics, concerts, parties, birthdays, and any other collection of reasons one could imagine, JoAnne thought of them. Her efforts paid off, as I moved to an apartment closer to my school where I could begin to host parties and dinners for JoAnne and David and, of course, for Randy as well.

Because Randy had been living in Baltimore where he used public transportation, he had no need to have a car and never had learned to drive. I would often pick him up at the end of the bus line that came out from the city and then drive him back to the city as well. But, in good time, Randy decided it was time for him to get a driver's license and perhaps get a car. The time was right. He signed up with a driving school, studied, practiced, passed the tests, got his license, and bought a Plymouth Barracuda that he nicknamed "Fishy." I was elated.

I was never good at math.

Probably the most outrageous mistake I ever made happened when I was chairman of the Guidance Department at South Carroll High School in Carroll County Maryland. I was responsible for making up the Guidance Department's budget for the year. I called a meeting with all four counselors, the guidance secretary, and myself. We all had ideas for upgrades and improvements in the department's programs and activities. New computers, new stationary, ergonomic desk chairs, fees for Career Development Day, anti-racism trainings, and so much more. I tallied all the requests and came up with the total of $1,698,500.00. I submitted the budget to my supervisor, Dolly Snyder, thinking what a good job I had done, getting everyone's input into our department's needs.

Then the phone rang. It was Dolly.

"Judy, what kind of budget have you done? For the whole state of Maryland? I just need South Carroll's numbers!"

"What do you mean, Dolly?" I said. "That's what I did."

"Judy," she said patiently. "I think you need to go back and add up your figures again. More than one million dollars is a bit much for one school's guidance department."

"What?? One million?? That cannot be right," I said.

"My thoughts, exactly!" said Dolly.

After checking my numbers and using an adding machine to arrive at the total costs, I had so much egg on my face that I could barely get myself to call Dolly back to explain that I had put the decimal point in the wrong place and that the total should have been $ 1,698.50.

"That's more like it," she said.

I didn't lose my job, but there were a lot of jokes flying around about my math deficits.

I still have trouble figuring out the time when standard time changes to daylight savings time. Yes, it's "fall back" and "spring forward," but what does that translate to on the clock face? If I go to bed at 11 o'clock, what time will it be when I wake up? Will I wake up? And since my husband is a clock collector, and we have 15 clocks in our house, it takes hours to re-set all of them.

I have resorted to looking at my cell phone which has

a clock face icon that tells me the time, and when I tap that clock face I am linked to the "world clock" which gives me the time in cities throughout the world, starting with Cupertino - 3 hours; New York +0; London +5; and Seattle -3. I must look up Cupertino to see why it has been given a starting place on the world clock list. And so, "google" takes me to Cupertino, a city in California, in the Pacific Time Zone. A click on to the world clock link brings me to a listing of many, many cities around the world with the time in each of those places. So now, when I get stuck with what time it is, all I have to do is click on the clock icon on my phone to find out what time it is in Cupertino and the rest of the world. Amazing technology but that still does not help me to know what time it is when I wake up and do not have my cell phone handy-by.

Perhaps I can blame my dilemma on my algebra teacher, or on my fourth grade teacher, or my forgetfulness, or my husband who thinks I should be able to calculate time in my head without using my fingers to count, or on the world clock, or on the first clock maker, or on daylight savings time itself.

So there we are with the concept of time, that thing that we use a clock or calendar to measure. We give time a number which presents a concept. That concept is both physical (January is winter and the temperature reads 28 degrees Fahrenheit) and subjective (my skin feels cold in January in Maine in the USA). Since ancient times (there's that word again), thinkers of the day have analyzed the concept of time. Plato, Aristotle, Newton, Einstein, and many more have put their stamp on the discussion of time. Not being in the same league as these philosophers, I can only say that I still can't calculate what time it is when we switch from standard time to daylight savings time. My sundial does not tell me. The grandfather clock does not tell me. My internal body clock does not tell me.

But the concept of time does tell me that events happen in a particular moment, and they last a particular duration. My optic neuritis happened in a particular month and year and lasted a particular length of time (can't escape that word). So even though I am a terrible math student, I can measure the length of an exacerbation of my MS (a physical concept of time) and can consciously understand that experience (subjective concept of time). So my life has been filling with a series of moments, or time capsules, of the duration of experiences over months and years. And, so, too, do most of us record those moments with notations on our desk calendars, or with photographs taken with our cell phones, or mental notations of life events, or maps of the locations of where we've lived or where we've traveled, or with lists of doctors we've seen or medications we've tried, or clothing we've worn, or pets we've had, or books we've read. Any numbers of things allow us to remember and to mark our time on this earth.

Randy invited me to a number of events at his apartment in the Bolton Hill section of the city of Baltimore. That area was filled with old brownstones which had mostly been converted to apartments but retained their glorious architectural details from the past. Randy's apartment was no exception. Enormously high ceilings, windows that practically skimmed the floor, large front rooms that could hold 15-foot Christmas trees, grand pianos and three manual electronic organs, sofas stuffed with horsehair and upholstered in antique green damask, couches covered with pale green satin, and drapes that fell in swoops from the ceilings to the floor. Elegant was the adjective!

Because Randy and I had gotten into a much closer relationship, I was drawn back into activities that we could share. Along with being a music teacher in the Baltimore City Public Schools, Randy was a church organist and choir director. Since I had grown up attending an Episcopal Church in Farmingdale, New York, a connection to church choirs and musical activities was very natural.

After a number of months spent driving from the suburbs of Carroll County into the city of Baltimore, I decided that it made sense for me to recalculate and move once again, this time into the city so Randy and I could be closer together. I found a lovely fourth floor walk-up apartment in Bolton Hill, the entire fourth floor of a gracious brownstone. With help from Randy and an army of assorted friends, I got moved to my 1500 Park Avenue apartment. What an address! 1500 Park Avenue! My rainbow café curtains found a spot on the window in the kitchen's eating area. My furniture was easily accommodated in the apartment, and I was settled, even though I now had a 45 minute commute to my school job in Carroll County.

By this time I had adopted two Siamese cats—Abigail and John. To prevent their bolting out a fourth floor window, Randy engineered chicken wire across the kitchen window so I could have the window open but the cats could not escape. There was no air conditioning. My cookbooks filled the shelf unit and pots and pans filled the kitchen cabinets. I started to have Randy over for dinner at least four or five times a week. One of our favorite suppers was tuna noodle casserole because there were often leftovers for a second supper. Things seemed to be getting serious. We even purchased a washing machine together that would be housed in the basement of Randy's building. That began a weekly date so that I could do my laundry and then cart the wet wash back to my fourth floor walkup apartment where I would hang it all to dry on clotheslines strung all through the apartment, like strings of Christmas tree lights. It is amazing how you can come up with inexpensive solutions to problems with a bit of inspiration and hard work! When the laundry was hanging in the apartment, the scent of wet clean clothes made me think of the laundry on the back yard clotheslines at my childhood home on Long Island.

One day Randy called and asked, "What's for supper?"

"Tuna noodle casserole leftovers."

"I'll be over in 20 minutes."

He arrived and found me sitting on the green sofa in the living room, the yellow and white oblong Pyrex casserole dish on my lap.

"Grab a fork," I said.

He did, and then sat down beside me.

"Will you marry me?" he asked as we shared our cold tuna-noodle casserole.

"Of course I will. I thought you'd never ask," I said.

"Let's look for a ring on Saturday, OK?" he asked.

That began the year of our engagement with meetings with the bishop to get approval so we could marry in the church, because I was a divorced woman.

With patience and forbearance, we finally arrived at our wedding day, the Feast of St. Michael and All Angels, September 29, 1973. I had commissioned a lovely seamstress in Baltimore to sew my wedding dress of off-white satin. I had a lace mantilla for a veil and satin shoes with a two-inch heel. I chose deep blue and purple Michaelmas Daisies as my flowers to commemorate the feast day of the angels. JoAnne, our Yente, was my Best Lady Matron of Honor, and David, her compatriot, was Best Man. We had a beautiful Nuptial Mass uniting Randy and me in the Sacrament of Holy Matrimony at the multi-racial Episcopal Church of St. Mary the Virgin, Baltimore, Maryland. Father Lloyd George performed the ceremony, and the wonderful church choir and acolytes assisted. We had invited the entire congregation to the wedding and the reception at the Eichenkranz Restaurant and Singing Society in South Baltimore. Randy and I were so happy that many members of our families, friends from our jobs, and various friends from school days and church connections were able to attend the ceremony and festivities.

We had a brief, three-day honeymoon over the week-end because we could not get extra time off from our jobs. We drove to Atlantic City and checked into a two-star hotel where we discovered too late that there were bed bugs! A quick exit the next morning and we headed south to the seaside resort town of Cape May and a delightful two days at a lovely and clean Bed and Breakfast. We spent time walking on the beach, exploring the Washington Street Pedestrian Mall with its shops and restaurants, and admiring the famous grand Victorian houses. This first honeymoon would be supplanted in the future by trips to Great Britain, Italy and many additional places in the United States. But this first honeymoon served to solidify our desire to be travelers, not just tourists.

We had secured a new apartment at the Carlyle, a multi-story new apartment building in the Roland Park neighborhood of Baltimore. I moved from 1500 Park Avenue to 500 S. University Parkway and he moved from his Lanvale Street apartment. I kept wondering what other "500s" would there be in my life!! We had our two cats, Abigail and John Adams. We had lovely space, huge windows overlooking the city, plenty of space for our desks and books and for Randy's grand piano which had been hoisted upside-down up to the fifth floor on top of the elevator. Our kitchen was tiny but had space enough for cooking. We had a small outdoor deck and plenty of closet space. Only once did Abigail escape and go meandering down the hall with Randy and me chasing her chanting "here, kitty, kitty" as if it were a liturgical response during a mass. She finally turned around and we snatched her, praying none of our neighbors reported us for disturbing the peace.

Chapter Eleven
Moving to Vermont

After our wedding, living in our sumptuous Baltimore high rise apartment with the Seoul Korean Restaurant on the ground floor, Randy and I thought very seriously about moving out of the city. We were ready to recalculate! We considered moving to Australia, but found that you needed to have a job in place before you would be allowed to emigrate. Also, we had elderly parents and did not want to be so far that we could not get back in a relatively reasonable time. So we looked at many different places in the United States. Having traveled several times to New England, we decided we would explore opportunities in those beautiful states. We sent out over 500 letters of inquiry with our resumes to school districts in Massachusetts, Vermont, New Hampshire, Maine, Rhode Island and Connecticut.

After what seemed like an interminably long time of waiting and getting replies of "no job vacancies," we finally received a reply from a district in Southern Vermont that was very encouraging. Randy could have a job teaching music at a junior high in Bennington and I could have a job teaching English in Arlington, a small town about a 20 minute drive north of Bennington. We were definitely re-calculating. We drove to Bennington and to Arlington for interviews and actually were hired. It was beautiful. What a change and what a chance for new directions. After the interviews and final hiring, we stayed a few extra days in Bennington to survey the area and talk with a real estate agent. He showed us several properties that we could manage in our price range. Talk about planning!!

We went back to Baltimore and began to get our financial house in order so we could purchase a house in Bennington. Randy's parents and my father each chipped in a little bit as a loan so we could make the down payment. The time was both busy and exciting. Leaving friends in Baltimore and looking forward to a new life in Vermont was absolutely mind boggling. We drove again to Bennington to finalize our house purchase and put the final touches on our new employment. It is a good thing that I do not mind mountains of paperwork or financial forms. We had a new bank and a mortgage and a house and new jobs. Life was so good.

We moved to Bennington in June of 1974 and began our new jobs in September. Our new house, a fixer-upper, was a four-bedroom, two-bath ranch home with a one car garage and a shallow cement front porch. We arrived with our two cars packed to the gills with belongings—I had the cats in my car and Randy had all the clocks in his car. On our trip up I-95 we tried to stay reasonably close together. My tunes were cat meows and Randy's tunes were ticking clocks.

We arrived on a Sunday afternoon and found that the previous owners had not removed all of their old over-stuffed furniture. The old green carpeting in the living room was stained and reeked of pet urine. We obviously had work to do before the moving van arrived from Baltimore the next two weeks. We decided to stay in the house that night and slept on the floor in the bedroom behind the garage since it did not have any of the smelly carpeting. We had a few blankets and a couple of pillows that we had crammed in the cars.

We had settled to sleep about 10 p.m. when we heard some scratching and noises coming from under the floor boards. Not one to take a liking to uninvited guests, I screamed bloody murder. I shook Randy and we gathered up the blankets to figure out what we had in the house with us. There was a small hole in the wooden flooring and we covered it with my ancient hard case Samsonite suitcase and piled a ton of books and heavy objects on top of that and tried to get back to sleep. In the morning we found the suitcase had been gnawed at by something with sharp teeth. After discovering little pellets in other places in the house, we figured that indeed we had a family of mice living with us.

That was the first and last night we spent in the house prior to clean up. We spent a few nights in the motel about two blocks away and went back to the house during the days to exterminate the mice and get rid of the smelly carpet and disgusting overstuffed furniture. This house would turn out to be the first of many on which we would put our stamp of renovation. Cleaning and painting and sanding the floors, purchasing a new refrigerator and a new stove and taking stuff to the dump occupied us for the two weeks before the United Moving Van arrived with all our stuff. I was feeling energized and prime for getting our house set to rights.

One of the first things to be unloaded was the washing machine that had previously lived in the basement of Randy's apartment building. No longer would I have to trek wet laundry two blocks though city streets and haul it up four flights of stairs and hang it up on lines strung throughout my apartment. No, now we could hang it outdoors on the spinner drying line where the wash would absorb sun and wonderful fresh air scents. Next were Randy's grand piano and our bedroom furniture, our dining room table and chairs, our green velvet sofa and red velvet swivel chair, two rattan chairs from the *Wizard of Oz* cast party, a vintage metal-top table for the kitchen, assorted wooden chairs, clothes, desks, my sewing machine, Christmas decorations, pots, pans, dinnerware, glassware, and everything else that we had accumulated in our combined 60 years of life.

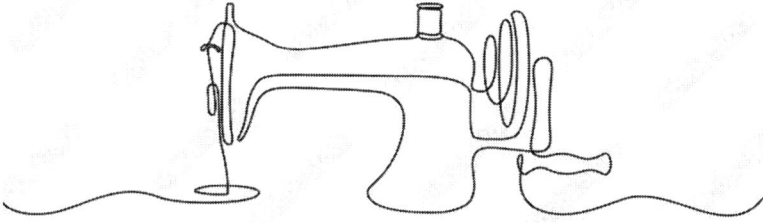

Chapter Twelve
Sewing, Cooking and Other Domestic Arts

When I was five years old, my mother gave me a tiny chain-stitching sewing machine. It had one needle that went up and down as I turned the rotary handle. There was no bobbin and just one post where the thread sat on the top of the machine. I suppose it was considered a toy in 1947, but I thought it was a real sewing machine. It was such a thrill to watch my mother sew and then try to emulate her. It was one of the ways that my mother and I connected. Shared experience is so important.

Now in 2021, I still have that little antique machine, just about five inches high and about seven inches side to side. The silvertone rotary handle is worn down to black metal in several spots. The machine now sits on the top shelf of a bookcase where books like Kate Greenaway's doll patterns and Small Quilting Projects now lodge and summon me to take up sewing once again. I now have a Husqvarna Viking computerized sewing and embroidery machine that keeps beckoning to me to try just one more project, but unfortunately, my MS keeps me from the sewing projects. I do not have the leg strength to stand at a table to cut patterns and put together quilt pieces. This is one of my great sadnesses. Since moving from Bennington in 2010, I have crafted some quilted place mats and put together a quilt using some Sunflower Sue and Overall Sam blocks that had been given to me a few years ago. I also crafted some Krumcake dolls that I donated to the church's Meals on Wheels Program so the seniors could give the six inch dolls to grandchildren.

I made the little dolls from felt, so I did not have to overcast the edges to prevent fraying. I used many shades of felt to simulate a variety of skin tones, and different materials for many kinds of hair textures and styles. My husband was in the middle of discarding ties that had seen better days and were out of date because they were too wide or too skinny. I commandeered the discarded ties and took them apart so I could use the fabric to make simple dresses for the Krumcake Kids. I threaded narrow ribbon through the folded over necklines so the ribbons could be tied at the shoulders for a custom fit. Before I sewed the back and the front of the dolls together, I embroidered a face on the front side. The dolls had smiles, puckered lips, wide open mouths, and different eyes that gave them personality. I think the creation of those Krumcake Kids was one of the most rewarding projects I have ever undertaken. I had baskets of these little dolls; they were like so many tiny kindergartners, stuffed together in one class.

Over the years, the dolls I have made have been the children I never had. The dolls I gave away were the best ones because they were priceless. I gave each doll a name.

Amanda had blonde curly hair and was dressed in a pink striped jump suit. Anna Rose, wearing a red print pinafore over a white blouse, had dark hair pulled back into a bun. She reminded me of my Nonna. Wearing a straw hat with tiny dried flowers, Madeline Nicole was the picture of a French mademoiselle, dressed in a pink ruffled dress with mutton sleeves. She even had her brown hair smoothed back into a chignon. Hannah wore a hand embroidered muslin dress with an antique lace collar. Charlotte Amanda was the picture of a Southern belle, wearing a pink chintz floor-length ball gown with ruffled lace at the hem and a big bow in her curly blonde hair. The dolls were my family.

I thought of writing children's books to feature each doll having an unusual adventure, but I never followed through with that idea. I think life got in the way.

From my mother's love of and talent for sewing, I gained perspective and skills that have been in my fingers and in my spirit for my whole life. When I graduated to using my mother's Singer sewing machine, I was using a machine that had created my sister Linda's Puss in Boots costume for Halloween in 1952. My sister wore that costume proudly and brandished the tri-cornered hat with its formidable feathers that encircled her little face. The boots that the Puss wore were fashioned of strips of black patent leather that fit over black patent leather shoes.

My mother's skill at costume creation also transferred to the costumes she and my godmother Aunt Virginia created for Rita's Dancing School in Freeport where my sister and I took dancing lessons for many years.

One year, Linda performed in a tap dancing routine called the Hat Box. The patent leather costumes were made with tops and skirts that were held up by underskirts of red tulle. The dancers had hats that looked like hat boxes that were made from cardboard covered with patent leather and lengths of red tulle that went over the hats and tied under the chin.

My mother's connection with Rita's Dancing School continued for several years as I took ballet classes and danced in many of the recitals that were put on at Rita's. I remember being a bumblebee and wearing the yellow dance costume with its short flip skirt and the wings that my mother fashioned from stiffened tulle painted with orange and blue and green to outline the veins of the wings. Another costume my mother sewed for me was for my sixth grade talent show presentation. I danced my Moon Maiden dance to Claude Debussey's *Clair du lune.* I wore my toe shoes and danced across the sixth grade stage after my teacher Miss Bullis put on the recording of *Clair du lune.*

The following poem was inspired by that sixth grade performance.

Moonshadow

The tarnished silver linings of clouds
Are gray with the ghosts of lost dreams,
Smoky mirrors, souvenirs of an old life.
The moon's crescent extends
A helping hook as if to lift me
From earthly constraints
To new vulnerabilities.
The moon maiden that once danced
Pirouettes and pliés
Now showers phantom specters
Of luminescent afterglow
On vestiges of a fading light.

Judith Krum, 2021

At Marietta College in the 1960s, I majored in English and minored in Education and in Speech and Drama. A favorite in the Speech and Drama department was a class in costume design and construction. Right up my alley. In one of the college buildings, a large basement room had been converted into a costume studio. I loved going down there and working the old treadle machines to construct costumes for whatever was the current college production. There were usually three productions each year so designing and making costumes was on-going. I think my mother would have been proud of my sewing and construction skills. That entire college class reminded me of the costume creations for Rita's Dancing School and the way my mother and my godmother designed and sewed hundreds of costumes.

My love of sewing has been part of me, practically for-ever.

I think I have always had a huge cache of fabric and sewing notions. Bags of zippers of all sizes and uses, jars of buttons collected from various people and places. I haunted garage sales for used clothing I could cut buttons off and tag sales that advertised antique linens and lace, and baby shoes that would fit some of my dolls.

As a teenager, I sewed many of my own clothes, from my poodle skirt to my Girl Scout uniform to a red pants suit I wore on my shortened honey moon to Atlantic City in 1973. From my mother I inherited a binder of sewing samples that she produced in her home economics class back in the 1920s and 30s.

There were samples of hemming darning, lace attachment, button holes, overcasting, and so many more sewing techniques. I am in awe of how she was able to learn and actually perfect all those various sewing skills. My mother also gave me a collection of Penny Squares that she and her sisters and friends embroidered back in the 1920s and 30s. Penny squares, which actually cost a penny, were muslin squares stamped with designs that could then be embroidered by hand. The Penny Squares were also called Redwork Squares because they were stamped with red ink and then embroidered with red embroidery floss. The designs I loved the most in my mother's collection were flowers, nursery rhymes, pithy sayings, small toys, and children.

After the fire in our North Bennington house in 1995, I had to go through all the rubble and remnants of my sewing supplies. When I saw the smoke damage and dark stains on those antique Penny Squares, I collapsed to the floor weeping. I felt like I had tarnished my mother's memory and had blemished her talent. This was a very bitter pill. Such a waste of all that talent and history. I tried all kinds of methods to get rid of the smoke stains and the noxious smell of the fire. Soaking them in bleach did not work because it just

At left, Judy (right) with the "redwork" quilt she made for her sister, shown here on the left.

Below is one of the "bridal bunnies" the author made during her days as a doll maker.

Pictured below, the Betty Crocker "Heart and Hearth" award Judy won as a high school student.

turned the muslin yellow and the red embroidery thread a light pink or white. It was disastrous.

By recalculating, I then began to look at the squares in a new way. I found some that had stains only on edges, leaving the design area fairly usable. I put piles of squares together by design style and by the edge that had damage. I decided I would sew pillows with ruffled edges for my four nieces. There were four salvageable squares that I could put in the center of each pillow by expanding the size with strips of additional red fabric like is done with quilting. These pillows became Christmas presents.

The other way that I used those stained Redwork squares was by making a large quilt for my sister. I cut away much of each damaged square and then sewed the remaining pieces onto red fabric that I pieced together for the quilt. I hand tied the quilt with short pieces of white yarn. I was so very happy that I had saved a bit of my mother's history for my sister as well as for my own peace of mind. That Christmas was an extremely happy one.

From then on I was determined to keep sewing and making gifts for all of my family. When the great nieces and great nephews came along, I celebrated their arrivals with many different types of stuffed animals and dolls and floor sitters.

Raggedy Ann and Andy for my eldest great niece, and a blue plush sit on dinosaur for my eldest great nephew

There was an embroidered quilt for another great niece and a sit-on lady bug for another one. A soft felt stuffed cow for still another, and a soft book with learning pages for the youngest great niece, as well as an animeko crocheted cat.

I fashioned another quilt using fabric strips that were given to me by a woman who could no longer use her sewing machine. This quilt I made while living in the apartment in Bennington as we were trying to sell our house and move to Florida.

Another woman at church was experienced with a long arm quilting machine so she machine-quilted what I named the Monet quilt because the yellow and blue colors made me think of Monet's *Garden at Giverny*. I gave the quilt to my church to be sold at the Christmas Craft shop.

I put together Overall Sam squares that had been given to me back in the 1990s. They were so cute, with their sun hats covering their heads and a handkerchief sticking out from the back overall pocket. I added borders and additional quilt squares.

We painted a feature wall in my craft room colors so the Overall Sam quilt would be reinforced.

One of my favorite quilts is one I made for Randy as a nap quilt. It is a blue and red and white quilt that has sailboats placed in vertical lines up and down the quilt. It is just the right size for a light warming while napping in a recliner chair. He still uses it now in 2021, though some spots are beginning to show wear. After all, it is more than 20 years old!

Back in high school I was named "Betty Crocker Homemaker of the Year" for my school; many of my classmates were a bit angry at me because I did not take home economics classes like they did. I had learned everything from my mother. When the Betty Crocker exam was announced, I signed up to take it. And I won with the highest score. This heart and hearth pin was awarded to the girl who scored the highest on a test of various homemaking skills, like cooking, sewing, health, child care, etc. That was before it was thought that girls could do things besides homemaking.

In 1995, after having retired from teaching, I was looking for new ways that I might earn some money and contribute to the household income. I was also still coming to terms with my infertility and from rejection by the adopted children.

The pillows shown above were made from squares of fabric known as "redwork" for their red stitching. They were also called "penney squares," their original price. Left above, Overall Sam squares were transformed into a quilt.

The boat themed quilt, top right, was made for the author's husband Randy. Cloth dolls, above and above left, were among her favorite projects. It all led eventually to a booth at the Crafters Outlet.

Besides creating gifts for family and friends, I rented a booth at the Cape Cod Crafter's Outlet in Manchester, Vermont.

My hope was that I could earn enough to at least cover the rental charge. I went to tag sales and auctions to gather small and old items that I could use in my booth to enhance the display of my crafts. I found small, old building blocks, some tiny stuffed animal toys, several old children's books, and at an auction, I bid on and got a little toy piano. I also used my antique child's sewing machine. I was just about set for the display. I had assembled many, many artificial flowers, tiny toy baby carriages, lots of metal doll stands, piles of my new business card "Buttercups," small baskets that the dolls could carry, tags to attach to the arms of the dolls giving their name, price, and any pertinent details about their construction.

Now I just needed enough dolls to complete the booth's vignette. I purchased yards of muslin and found some doll patterns for free on several websites. I purchased books on dollmaking and on how to create various kinds of hair and hair styles. Yarn was a favorite medium for hair, but also packages of mohair were available as well as ringlets of polyester that made really fun hair. I had to learn what kind of hair went with the many sorts of doll personalities I was creating. I learned how to embroider eyes and lips and to sculpt faces to give them dimension. I frequented sales at Michaels and other craft stores where I found hats and shoes and baskets and little toy bears and other little animals.

By this time I had cut out at least 50 doll bodies and doll limbs and heads and had sewn together many parts of doll anatomy. Everywhere I went I carried a bag of polyester fiberfill, assorted doll parts, and a wooden stick so I could stuff fiberfill into all the nooks and crannies of doll appendages. When Randy and I went on a road trip, I stuffed the dolls. When I went to a meeting, I carried my bag of doll stuffing and doll parts and stuffed doll parts, so that when I returned home to my sewing machine, I could do any machine embroidery I needed to do and then could sew the doll parts together. The hair material and style came next. An adult doll or a child doll, a girl or a boy, so many decisions had to be made. That was part of the fun of dollmaking.

Then I started making dolls.

I dressed the dolls in clothing I picked up at garage sales along with pieces I sewed myself. Garage sale shoes were the best because they were real shoes. Sometimes I could even find tights and socks that added to the reality of the dolls. Two of my favorites were Eloise and Eddie. They were large toddler dolls that stood about 23 inches tall.

Eloise wore a blue pinafore I sewed that went over a pink polka dot dress. She had striped pantaloons and real baby tights with embroidered hearts. She also had pink socks and real leather sandals. Her brown yarn hair was styled in two pony tails.

Eddie, was a hand crafted 23 inch boy doll, with needle sculpted face, wearing a shirt with buttons, pants, suspenders, a newsboy-type cap, and real toddler shoes.

I also made bridal bunnies.

I created wedding dresses for the bunnies from antique linens that had come down to me from my forbears as well as from Randy's family. I gave the bridal bunnies to nieces at their bridal showers. I think by this time I was beginning to realize that I was never going to plan weddings or create real wedding gowns for real children. This bitter pill still sticks in my throat.

My parents encouraged me to cook for the family and to make dinner most nights. When I was in high school, my mother went back to work so she appreciated my cooking abilities. My father also taught me many cooking skills that he had learned from his mother, my Nonna. Risotto was a favorite and so was 'the sauce," that could be used on all sorts of pasta dishes. He was the one who made the stuffing for the Thanksgiving turkey. I still know the recipe by heart, though sadly, I am not able to cook any more myself. The turkey stuffing was made with Italian bread cubes soaked in milk, frozen chopped spinach cooked and squeezed practically dry, sweet Italian sausage and ground hamburger meat all frizzled together with chopped onion and lots of herbs like thyme and rosemary. It was like a casserole. It was so good.

In the 1970s when Randy and I were getting to know each other, I tempted him with dinners and cooking that he loved. The first Thanksgiving dinner we were together, I invited him to my apartment in Manchester, Maryland. I had prepared a full turkey dinner (with my father's turkey stuffing), green bean casserole, sweet potatoes, mashed potatoes, turnips, and a pumpkin chiffon pie flavored with Cointreau. I think that sealed the deal and proved the old saying that "the way to a man's heart is through his stomach."

After we got married, I continued to do much of the cooking, although Randy liked to cook as well and had been cooking for himself for many years before we were married. And now in 2021, as I have become more and more disabled, cooking and baking are occupations that I am very sad for having lost. I remember the smooth feel of pastry dough as I made flaky Danish pastries. Swedish Spritz butter cookies are no longer offered to visitors at Christmas. I no longer can engineer a lovely pot roast and roasted vegetable dinner. I find that meals now are mostly ready-made and microwaveable or delivered from favorite restaurants. But we do not go hungry, and I am grateful for that and for my husband who now shoulders most of the household responsibilities as well as taking care of me.

Chapter Thirteen
Adopting a Sibling Group

"MOM, IT'S ME, MARY," she cried from beneath her Halloween mask. "Don't you know me?" They had never been trick or treating before. Mary was five, John was six, and Richard was seven. The sibling group knew their names and their backgrounds. They had known their biological parents and family. We adopted them from an orphanage in Massachusetts where they had been placed because of child neglect.

We desperately wanted a family and these kids seemed tailor made to become the children who could become our family. I so desperately wanted to be a mother. I knew it was not going to be possible for me to get pregnant, so after much discussion and soul-searching we decided to go down the path of adoption. There are so many kids who need homes, who need opportunity, who need "us," or so we thought.

In 1976, we embarked on a path filled with of social workers, detailed questionnaires, psychological interrogations, financial inspections, home inspections, education reviews, reviews of extended family, and so much more to determine if we would be fit parents. I felt as if we were undergoing a vetting for a spot on the Supreme Court or at least on the TV show *You Bet Your life*.

After many discussions with our social worker from the orphanage, it was determined that we would do best with an older sibling group. We were both involved in our jobs and did not want to give up working. At 33 and 34, we were well beyond the age when most people become first parents and are looking forward to changing diapers and sterilizing baby bottles. We did not want to be in our 70s when the kids were in their 20s. So an older group seemed most likely to be a good "fit." There were so many older kids who had been deemed unadoptable because of age or circumstance.

The social worker went through a long list of challenges that an older group would present to us. Kids might be children of drug addicts and would have serious psychological and learning disabilities. Some kids had been diagnosed with fetal alcohol syndrome and had learning and physical disabilities. Some of the kids had attachment disorders and seemed less able to bond with new parents. Many remembered their birth families and might want to return to them at some point. Sometimes, sibling groups were so bonded with each other that they did not want anyone else to intrude on their perceived family group. Some of the kids had shown tendencies to act out and to hurt themselves or others.

There was so much to consider. Were we ready? Did we have the love and fortitude to embark on this journey? Were we strong enough in our marriage to accept a sibling group of kids into our family and to truly accept them as our kids? There was so much discussion and soul searching.

Finally we made the decision to go ahead with the adoption process. The social worker first had us visit the kids at the orphanage to see if we could be a good match. We drove to Massachusetts and visited the children at the orphanage, a low gray building with several wings expanding from the center, and a playground that looked like a typical elementary school playground with swings, see-saw, and a large asphalt space for playing kickball and other sports. I found the exterior rather depressing: Gray, hard surfaces, fences, and a rather unwelcoming entrance. I was wondering how kids could find any softness in such a place.

We parked in a visitors parking space and followed signs to the office. Once inside, I could sense a different atmosphere. The interior was painted with bright colors and child-friendly furniture was evident. We met our social worker who took us to the dining room, a sort of school cafeteria space. Another social worker brought the three kids into the room. They were at once shy and cautious. We engaged them in conversation about themselves, their names, what they liked to do, where they went to school, what they liked to eat, all the things we could think of to get them more at ease and comfortable with us.

Richard liked to watch wrestling and boxing and thought he might like to become a policeman. John liked to play video games and thought he might like to have a dog. Mary said she liked to play with Play-Doh and might like to learn to ride a horse. They all expressed interest in having us come for another visit sometime so we could go out to McDonald's for a lunch. We said we would be making arrangements to do that.

The second visit was about a month later. We were all set to take them out to a local McDonald's, the beacon for kids of all ages. The kids warmed up to us fairly quickly and ordered the standard kids' meals. It was interesting to watch the dynamics among the three. Richard, the eldest, sort of took charge and told the other two what to do and where to go and where to sit. John and Mary took cues from Richard and also asked Randy and me questions about where we lived and what we did. After about an hour we took the kids aback to the orphanage. They were anxious to show us where they lived and where their rooms were. Randy and I made arrangements for another visit when we would take the kids back to our house for an overnight visit and talk with them about school and friends and what they were hoping for.

After several visits, we finally took the kids into our family. I won't deny; it was a tough transition for all of us. They got registered for school. We developed a fairly organized home routine. Bus schedules. Lunches. Clothes. We hired a baby sitter/nanny to supervise the kids afternoons before Randy and I got home from work.

Our home on Merson Street in Bennington was perfect. It had four bedrooms, two bathrooms, a big yard, and lots of opportunities to socialize with other kids in the neighborhood.

My husband and I continued our teaching careers. We got the kids enrolled in schools. Mary qualified for "special ed" because of mild mental retardation from the fetal alcohol syndrome caused by her biological mother. John was enrolled in first grade and Richard in grade three. They were all in public schools in Bennington. We scheduled the nanny to be at our home from noon to 4 p.m. each day, so she'd be there when Mary came home on her bus from her half-day kindergarten session and when the boys came home from school at 2:30 p.m. Our kids developed friendships with other kids in the neighborhood, and after a year had passed they seemed to be settling in to life as a family with us.

It was the autumn of 1976, the centennial celebration of the USA. In Bennington, Vermont, a huge host of activities were planned to commemorate the centennial. One of the major events was a big community-wide parade with folks dressed in garb reminiscent of 1776. I made outfits for the kids and for myself. Randy would wear the costume I had made for his participation in the musical play *1776* which had run during the three weeks before the big celebration.

All dressed up, we headed the three blocks on foot down to Main Street to join the throngs of parade watchers. The kids all had 1776 flags, and we waved them as the fire trucks and various community organizations went by —the Boy Scouts, Girl Scouts, the high school marching band, and numerous state and local officials and dignitaries. Floats had been created by the Future Farmers of America, the DAR, the VFW, and several other groups. It was a true home town, grass roots celebration. The parade wound around town and ended up finishing at the Bennington Battle Monument, a 306-foot-high stone obelisk located at Monument Circle. The monument commemorates the Battle of Bennington during the American Revolutionary War. Fife and drums corps performed as well as ensembles from the high school. The town's officials read from the Declaration of Independence.

We experienced our first Christmas as a family that year as we got a real tree from the local fire department, which was selling them at a community park. Getting the tree set up was a big deal for the kids as we believed it was their first real Christmas. Ornaments and tinsel were added, and a big star on the top. They helped to set up the crèche scene with wooden figures and animals and learned about the baby Jesus and the three wise men. We spent time looking through the old sears Christmas Toy catalogue and they had great fun picking out toys that they hoped Santa would bring them..I believe that was the first time they had ever done anything like that.

Of course, Randy and I were making note of all the toys they wanted and I ordered many of them and had them delivered to the home of one of Randy's music teacher colleagues so they could remain a secret to the last minute. Randy and I would take turns evenings to go over to Peter's house and wrap the presents. I guess we went a little overboard but the gifts were finally all wrapped a few days before Christmas, Then we had to figure out how we would get them to our house on Christmas Eve. Our friends were going away to their parents' houses for three days before and after Christmas, so they gave Randy their house key so he could go over and collect the gifts.

On Christmas Eve, Randy drove our big green station wagon over to collect the presents. It was about midnight because we had waited till our kids were fast asleep in their own beds. Randy parked in their driveway and turned off his car lights so as not to disturb the neighbors. He got out of the car and went up the back steps and opened the door. In about five minutes he had taken about five or six gifts to the car. That is when a policeman came to the door and wanted to know why Randy was removing gifts from this house and loading them into his car. It took a while to explain the situation and have the police call our friends to verify that this was legitimate and that we were not stealing presents. Apparently, Peter had not told his neighbors that this was going to happen and that it was okay. Randy did not get arrested. It did take him about10 trips back and forth to get all the presents, however.

At the Merson Street house, we were able to have a very large garden at the back of our property. Randy rented a rototiller and tilled the big plot of deep, rich soil. The earth was so rich that a pencil could have grown in it. We planted tomatoes and beans and cucumbers and zucchini and pumpkins. The kids seemed to enjoy helping things grow and took some pride in the harvest.

We also tried to find activities that the kids seemed interested in. In the town where I worked, Arlington, Vermont, there was a very active youth soccer program and I asked the director (one of my teaching colleagues) if our two boys would be able to participate even though they were not residents. I got the okay and the boys were thrilled. Randy and I took turns every Saturday driving them the half hour up to the Arlington Park. A number of my high school students worked as youth coaches and they were so friendly and skilled. John and Richard were put in two separate groups, separated by age and physical stature. John was quite a bit smaller than Richard and was almost two years younger. Soccer proved to be a good activity for the boys as they were both fond of running and were able to learn some of the footwork needed to get the soccer ball going in the right direction. Even now, almost 40 years later, my old students ask me on Facebook how the kids are doing.

While the boys were getting involved in soccer, Mary had expressed an interest in learning how to ride a horse. We found a stable about a 15 minute drive north of our house and investigated the possibility of Mary's learning to ride. It proved to be a good connection. Mary loved it and we found the teacher to be kind and able to work with Mary's learning deficiencies. Mary actually became pretty adept at riding and loved her riding outfit of jodhpurs and jacket and boots and velvet riding helmet. She rode in several shows and contests and earned several ribbons. We were proud of her and she was proud of herself. It seemed we were making progress.

In 1978, we found that a wonderful house in North Bennington was going on the market. The house had been the home of *Summer Sonatina*, a piano program for people of all ages and from all over the country and the world. Randy was acquainted with the family that started the program and knew that the father in the family was an organist and had installed a pipe organ in the dining room of the house. It was said that there was a piano, maybe even two, in every room of the house. One of the draws for that house was that it had a side entrance into a small room that could be a waiting room for parents who brought kids for piano lessons.

The house was a two-story plus attic home, with four bedrooms and lots of space. We had a huge flower garden along the front of the garage, but there was no room to grow vegetables. So we rented a quarter of an acre of land from the Park McCullough House and property about a block and a half from our house so we could get involved in growing vegetables. After all, it was the 70s and the "back to the land" movement was in full swing. We picked rocks and stones and tilled the earth with a rented rototiller. We laid out our plan for corn, peas, beans, peppers, cucumbers, zucchini, squash, pumpkins—whatever the kids wanted.

Things went along well for about a month; we had everything planted and were anticipating a bountiful harvest. The only problem was that there was no water. No hose connection. No well. And very little rain. We outfitted a little red wagon with two big metal pots, filled them with water at home, and pulled and pushed the wagon down to our little vegetable plot. Dispensing water to keep our vegetables alive became almost a full time job. But we persisted and actually harvested enough cucumbers so I could make pickles, and zucchini to make zucchini bread, a few pumpkins to decorate the porches of the house, a few peppers to make stuffed peppers. The corn was a disaster and the beans shriveled up and disintegrated. The garden was definitely not a Victory Garden like the ones during WWII.

We wanted the kids to become acquainted with their cousins on Long Island. My sister and her kids had come to Bennington to visit and meet our kids. From then on we arranged trips to get the cousins together. My sister and I would meet halfway on the Taconic Parkway and exchange children. Sometimes one or two of her three would go back to North Bennington with me, while one or two of my group would go back to Long Island with her. The exchange arrangement provided a kind of summer vacation experience for everyone. And the kids were able to feel part of a bigger family.

We drove to Florida and took our kids to Disney World. What else could we do to make them feel part of the great family dream?

As has happened throughout my life, there was another major recalculation. We had a house fire in the North Bennington house in 1985. Randy was at a music teachers' convention in Boston and I was home with Mary and John. Richard was grown and had moved to Montpelier with his girlfriend. That evening, Mary and I had gone to a pot luck Lenten supper at church and John stayed at home as his legs were hurting him. The doctor called them "growing pains." He used a heating pad on his legs to relieve the discomfort.

All of a sudden, in the middle of the pot luck dinner, our friend Bill came over to me and said there was a fire in our house! Oh my God!!! John was home. Was he okay? I asked all the folks at the pot luck to look after Mary, and I raced out of the church to my car with Deacon Penny close behind, and headed to North Bennington. There were numerous fire trucks at the house shooting water hoses up to the roof of the house. My heart sank. But then I saw John on the sidewalk watching everything and I raced over to hug him and make sure he was all right. He was talking to one of the firemen, telling him there were two cats and a dog in the house that he couldn't get to. But try as they did to rescue them, our pets perished from the smoke of the fire. Then Bill came from church — he was a member of the fire department — and they draped plastic sheeting over much of the contents on the first floor, including Randy's piano and his practice electronic organ.

The house was a disaster. Our priest called Randy in Boston and told him there had been a "small fire" at the house but everyone was okay, and that I would stay at the rectory that night. John was going to stay at the home of his Culinary Arts teacher, and Mary would stay at her friend's house, and that Randy should come to the rectory when he got back to Bennington. And thus began a year of recalculating. I walked through the charred remains of the house, in tears at the sight of smoke-stained books and antique linens, seeing our clothing charred and unusable, plastic sheets over musical instruments, the bathtub completely smoke-stained. What were we going to do?

We couldn't stay in the house. We were homeless. News of the house fire was the front page story in the local paper the next day. Offers of clothing and household linens came pouring in. Our church family helped us to collect stuff so we could at least have a change of clothes. One of the local doctors was away on vacation and he offered us the use of his house for two weeks. One of my Arlington colleagues offered us the use of their church building for several days.

Then came the terrible time of sifting through whatever we could find in the charred and smoky remains at the house. Pictures, antique redwork embroidery that had been passed down from my mother's family, files of Randy's music that had been accumulated for more than 50 years, my wedding dress, so much that was just irreplaceable. The insurance company came in and surveyed the damage. I had to make lists of everything we had lost, down to my sewing supplies like buttons and fabric. A cleaning company was hired to come in and clean whatever might be still useable. The insurance company gave us a settlement on our claim. Eventually we hired a contractor to make repairs and add a family room on to the east side of the house. Recalculating from this disaster took some time, but we did end up back in the house.

School seemed to go along fairly well although all the kids were having various learning and behavioral difficulties. We were frequent parents at IEP meetings that allowed the school to determine what accommodations were needed for each child to progress as well as possible. Learning difficulties were proving frustrating and difficult for all of them. John was having a hard time with holding a pencil and writing. The school tested him and found that he had dysgraphia as well as dyslexia. Unless one qualified for special education, school could be frustrating and very difficult. When he was about 14, we found a private school in Connecticut that specialized in helping kids with John's learning issues. He said he would go there for a while. He did attend for about a year, and then one day we got a call from their counselor who told us that John had started cutting himself and that he would be better served somewhere else. We brought him home and talked about what we should do. We spoke with John, and with the various staff members at the local junior and senior high school. What programs might help John learn as much as possible and help him become a self-sufficient young man who felt good about himself. He decided that the culinary arts program appealed to him and he wanted to try that. That proved a good move as the program gave him skills and bolstered his self confidence.

Mary also was having a hard time. She became frustrated at her lack of friends and her inability to keep up with school work as much as she would like to. Because she qualified for special education, she continued to have monitored classes and extra help all through high school. She eventually graduated with a modified diploma. However, she ran away from home for a few days and was brought back by the police who showed us that she had been shoplifting. After several tries at working with a psychologist and finding a job, she ran away again. That is when she was placed in a half-way house. As hard as we tried, we could not get her released into our custody.

Richard, then age 16, also had lots of behavioral problems. He did okay in school and academics were not a problem. But he acted out and picked fights with everyone. Again, working with a psychiatrist for some time did not prove helpful and Richard also got into trouble with police. He became violent at home also. One night when Randy was away at a school meeting, Richard came after me with a knife in the kitchen. I recall how I grabbed Mary and John and the dog and rushed them and me up to my bedroom on the second floor where I locked the door and braced it with a chair. I called police from the phone in the bedroom. They came and looked all over for Richard, finally finding him hiding in the garage.

I was so afraid. I was so ashamed. I was so debilitated by my failure to be the mother I had always wanted to be. I had no idea what would come next. I just knew that I didn't know what to do. Randy and I talked more and more about what options we could see. We contacted family counselors and our friends at church and at our schools. It was at this point that Mary had run away and been put in jail in Massachusetts. Richard had taken off from his judicial placement. John was living at home and had gotten his driver's license. We got him a car so he could go back and forth to work. But then John took off also. We got a phone call from him saying he had gone to Indiana and was living with Richard there. We tried to find Mary to see if we could help her with her judicial problems. When we found where she was and called the facility, we were told she had gone back to live with her biological parents and didn't want us to contact her. Eventually we also got a phone call from John saying he was living with Richard and Richard's wife and their kids and they were going to go back to using their biological last names and would be contacting their biological family as well.

"Please do not follow us," he said.

That seemed to me to be the end of a big chapter. And to this day, we have not had any contact

I just pray that the 10 years or so that they were with us and the love we showed them when they were our kids have been at least a comfort of some sort. I am still empty and sad about that chapter.

Chapter Fourteen

ADA Activism and a
Visit from NPR's John Hockenberry

It was 1994. Randy had joined the faculty at Hoosac School, a private boarding school about 10 miles west of Bennington. He was the music teacher and the Dean of Students and was musical director of the "Boar's Head and Yule Log" holiday pageant that had been produced at the school since 1892. I had retired from teaching in Arlington in 1990, as my MS was making it more difficult for me to get around. I was hoping to find another teaching job because I knew we could use the money, and I felt I still had it in me to continue to teach.

We became house parents for a boys dorm at Hoosac and I was hired to teach English and American Culture — a kind of social studies and civics class for the many international students who attended Hoosac. After several years at Hoosac, we started to look for different employment. It was becoming more and more difficult for me to travel between buildings that were not accessible. I sent applications to a number of school districts in upper New York State, and Randy was hired to set up the classical music department at the new Borders Books and Music that was opening in Albany, New York.

I received invitations from several school districts to interview for English teaching positions. But now that I look back on that time, I am thankful that I did not get hired—especially at places like Saranac Lake, New York, where winter temperatures dip to lows of -30 and where three-foot-high snow falls are common. What was I thinking? It was hard enough to get around in Bennington in the winter; how would I manage in the Adirondack Mountains? Recalculating one's career direction can sometimes uncover decisions that turn out to be less than desirable.

This also was the time that I became friends with a man in Bennington whose wife had MS. Charlie became a mentor and friend as I began to struggle more and more with my MS diagnosis. Through Charlie I became acquainted with the Vermont Center for Independent Living (VCIL), a private state-wide organization that was run by people with disabilities of all kinds and that served people with all kinds of disabilities. Charlie worked there. I was hired first as a Peer Advocate Counselor and then as a community organizer for compliance for the Americans with Disabilities Act. I think that my work with VCIL came at just the right time with me in just the right place. I was working through my new life as a person with a disability and was able to learn so much from my peers and colleagues at VCIL.

Because he was blind, Charlie had a driver who took us to our twice monthly meetings and trainings at the VCIL main office in Montpelier. VCIL is a cross-disability organization, so I was soon introduced to people who were blind, deaf, had psychological disabilities, were wheelchair users, had mental retardation, and a host of other disabilities. We had many people who had guide dogs and who used American Sign Language. I received such an important education from my work with VCIL. We opened a satellite office in Bennington and became a place for people to come for information about their rights as persons with disabilities. We did surveys of local business establishments to determine which places were complying with the ADA. We worked with the town government to ensure that people with disabilities were able to vote and to attend public meetings. We also worked with the Bennington Museum to help that facility install an elevator and a wheelchair accessible front entrance.

One of my favorite stories involves the time I caused a public meeting to be moved to an accessible location because it was being held on the second floor of a court building that had no elevator. I had gotten to the first floor via an interior lift that wheelchair users could use to get from the ground floor to the first floor, but no further. I sat in my wheelchair and watched the parade of temporarily able-bodied citizens walk past me and continue up the stairs to the second floor. Finally, my friend who had come with me went upstairs to inquire whether there was a secret elevator that I could use to get up to the meeting. No, indeed, there was not said the Town Clerk who was in charge of the meeting. The Town Clerk came down to talk to me to see what we could do to accommodate my needs. I said we could hold the meeting outside or at a different location, one that was wheelchair accessible. The Clerk said we would move the meeting to the firehouse, which was accessible. And next all the citizens who had climbed up the stairs to the second floor came streaming down and we all headed to the firehouse, about two blocks away. The Americans with Disabilities Act applies to access for town and state governments as well as retail establishments and other public accommodations. VCIL had taught me well. I could also remember Father Hampshire's words about his Prayer Pilgrimage and the dignity of every person.

Apparently my work with the ADA in Bennington somehow reached the ears of newscasters and news services in a wider area because one day, sort of out of the blue, I got a call from John Hockenberry, National Public Radio general assignment reporter. His list of awards included being an ABC News Emmy recipient, and a two-time Peabody Award winner. He was also author of *Moving Violations, A Memoir- War Zones, Wheelchairs, and Declarations of Independence (1995)*. John was on assignment to interview people in different parts of the country to find out how the Americans with Disabilities Act was being implemented. I was amazed and startled and felt very honored to be in John Hockenberry's radar. A cover story he wrote for the July 26th, 2005 issue of *Parade* magazine on the 15 year anniversary of the Americans With Disabilities Act reached 75 million readers.

We talked about motels and hotels in Bennington where he could stay when he came to town. The Paradise Motor Lodge was the best choice for "handicapped" accessibility. So I gave him the phone number and a little information about the Paradise. He would make his own reservation. He said he would call me when he arrived and then we could map out our plan to survey ADA compliance in Bennington. When he called, we agreed to meet in the parking lot of the Bennington Museum. I was sitting in my wheelchair in the parking lot when John arrived. The first thing I noticed when we met was that he was able to reach around from the driver's seat, grab his folded up wheelchair and swing it around parallel to the open driver's side car door, and then, by putting his hands on either side of his body on the driver's seat, he lifted himself up and over to sit in his wheelchair. I was astounded. I asked him how long it took to learn to master that flawless exit move. He said that it took lots of practice and exercises to increase his arm strength.

I thought to myself that I would never be able to swing myself out of the car and into my wheelchair without massive assistance. What I usually did was to drive myself to wherever I was going and then park and get out of my car on the driver's side. I would hold on to the car and side step myself to the rear of my PT Cruiser. Then I would open the hatchback and lift my wheelchair out of the car to the street. I could reach up to grab the hatch back and pull it down to close it. Then I could sit in my chair and roll myself to my final destination, hoping that there would not be much traffic and that there would be curb cuts when I needed to get up to the sidewalk from the street. If there was a steep curb cut or if I was going up a hill, I would need to roll myself backwards to maximize my arm strength. I could see from John's arm strength that I was going to have difficulty keeping up with him.

The following is an excerpt from an article by Judith Michaelson, July 3, 1995, in *the Los Angeles Times*.

"In 1976, Hockenberry was a student at the University of Chicago with plans to major in math, when he and his best friend hitched a ride with two female students. The driver fell asleep, as did Hockenberry in the back seat. He woke up just before the car hit a guardrail and plunged 200 feet over an embankment in Pennsylvania. The driver died, but Hockenberry's friend was not hurt. A truck driver with a fire extinguisher put out the flames before the car blew up. Hockenberry lost all sensation below his chest."

So, I figured that he'd had about 16 years of exercising and physical endurance training to get himself in such good shape. After all, he had traveled to the Middle East and had been involved in so many things that I had not even read about, let alone experienced.

We rolled to the main entrance of the museum and went in the front door. It was propped open, so we did not have to struggle with the heavy door like is usually the case for wheelchair users. I had previously called and made an appointment for us to meet with the museum director. The director talked about the changes and ADA improvements that had been done, not the least of which was an elevator so people with mobility difficulties could get to the second floor to see the many displays and artifacts housed there. John and I took advantage of the elevator and found it was very large, not only so wheelchair users could use it, but also so that large furniture pieces and art work could be lifted to the second floor. We pointed out that elevators are not only useful to people who use wheelchairs but to businesses as well. The director said that the Museum's Board of Directors was very aware of that fact, and it was one of the reasons that the elevator had been installed.

After our visit at the Museum, we headed down the hill to my house where we would take a rest and have some coffee. I was so glad that I had an accessible house with a wheelchair ramp on the front, leading right to the front door. How could I be an ADA advocate if my home were not welcoming to people with disabilities, and if wheelchair users could not get into the house?

Me (Judy) with John Hockenberry, noted journalist, author, Public Radio host, at the Krum dining room table in Bennington, Vermont, as John and I were about to tour downtown Bennington, talking with officials and citizens about the impact that the Americans with Disabilities Act had been having in Bennington, 2005.

After our respite and more conversation, we headed to a meeting with the Town Manager and the Town Clerk. The ADA applies to state and local government operations as well as to retail and medical businesses. Bennington had been making sure that voting venues were accessible to citizens with disabilities. The town office building was also accessible and, if requested, sign language interpreters could be provided. Other accommodations could also be provided to citizens with other disabilities. I was so proud of the work that I and other VCIL colleagues had accomplished.

Following our town meeting, John and I continued our tour of Main Street and checked for access to several stores and restaurants. Most establishments were ADA compliant and were happy to see us checking for that. One of the biggest problems was the ramp at the public library. It had been installed before the ADA guidelines were put in place and the ramp itself, though with the best intentions, was so steep that a person using a manual wheelchair would have to be pushed up the ramp or would have to pull themselves up by holding the metal pipe railing on the side of the building and go hand over hand to the top of the ramp.

As the day came to a close, John headed back to the Paradise Motor Inn and I headed back home. That was one of the most exhilarating days I have ever experienced since my MS diagnosis. Rolling through town with John, another wheelchair user, was an incredible builder of self-esteem. Besides, John had a manual "Quickie" wheelchair with no arm rests just like me. John and I had many opportunities to talk about the ADA. We agreed that the law started out as a civil rights act enforced by alleged victims of discrimination who filed lawsuits to force compliance. We both thought that was rather backwards. With the various exclusions built into the ADA and the phrase "undue burden" for many small businesses, we thought that enforcement of the ADA was lacking in "teeth" and did not have enough weight behind it. Though there had been some improvements for access, there was still much to get done. Workplace accommodations, public transit accommodations, educational accommodations, how people with disabilities are portrayed in film and entertainment, the public's expectations of people with disabilities, social acceptance, religious institutional acceptance, the whole concept of inclusion, the re-working of architectural design, and so many other ideas had to be discussed. We talked about how the ADA hits at the heart of the idea of inclusion. Do we want certain people to be excluded from mainstream life or not? That, my dear citizens, is the question. Recalculation had only just begun.

Chapter Fifteen
Moving to Florida

I was very sad about moving to Florida. All my friends were in Vermont. My home church was in Vermont. I had lived in Vermont for more than 35 years, and almost had become accepted as a "real" Vermonter. I felt my whole being lived in Vermont and would be drained of life and love if I moved to Florida. I had retired and was beginning to write again, something I had always dreamed of doing. Now I had time to pursue that dream. I had become a true wheelchair user and lived in a house that was accessible. We had a wheelchair access ramp installed on the front of the house, leading to the front door. It signaled that people with disabilities were welcome.

We also had a ramp inside the garage so I could enter the house directly from the car in the garage. Even the bathroom had been renovated to be a roll in shower. I even had a three-wheel scooter that I could use to go downtown and to church, at least in the spring and summer and fall. But in the winter I became housebound — frozen by the ice and snow that enveloped the whole area.

Discussing such a retirement move was almost always

a topic of discussion in our home. Randy was planning to retire from Southern Vermont College in 2010.. I was already retired. We both were eligible for Medicare and we each had a small retirement pension. With living costs and tax liability much less in Florida than in Vermont it seemed to be a fiscally prudent if not, to me, emotionally prudent thing to do. With my MS and its concurrent vision problems, I decided to give up my driver's license and we sold my car. Again the act of giving up and the feeling of loss was pervasive.

We set to figuring out how to get our Bennington house sold. Much work needed to be done to make it visually more appealing and physically more sound. We hired someone to put in a new automated garage door opener. We waterproofed the basement walls. A plumber improved some the piping that needed attention. We had kitchen renovations done to increase counter and storage space. New countertops were installed. Floors were sanded and stained and waxed. We rented a storage space where we could put items that made the house appear too cluttered.

Next was listing with a reputable Real Estate agent. We talked with several and finally decided on one we felt comfortable with regarding our asking price and the manner in which the house would be marketed. During the year that the house was on the market, we moved into a small apartment on the east side of town, which we found just by happenstance in the apartment listings of the local newspaper. The price was right; it had a flat wheelchair accessible front door, and the landlord approved our having a dog. There was a dishwasher, a stacked washer dryer, three bedrooms and a dining room, and we could change the purpose of any room to suit our needs. One bathroom even had a door that was wheelchair accessible and a bathtub that would accommodate equipment to allow me to bathe. We were in business!

Randy took the front bedroom where he set up blowup

mattresses for his bed, along with his computer equipment. The dining room became the music room containing the practice electronic organ. The big bedroom along the length of the house became our closet. Randy set up bunches of plastic coated wire sections to hold our clothing at heights I could reach from my wheelchair. But the big sundrenched back sun room with many, many windows all around on three sides of the room became my room. I could sleep comfortably in my recliner chair and spend lots of time shredding file documents that we no longer needed and had no reason to take to Florida. It was the perfect apartment for us as we began to draw away from our long time home in Bennington.

The year before we moved into the apartment, we drove our RV with my car attached behind, from Bennington to a campground in Orange City, Florida. The campground would be our home base for a few weeks while we looked at Florida housing possibilities. My old elementary school chum Susan had been encouraging us to settle in De-Land, the home of Stetson University. So we looked there and found a manufactured home community named Whisperwood that seemed very nice and affordable. They even had an area where owners could park and store their RVs. Plus we found St. Barnabas Episcopal Church in DeLand and instantly fell in love with that church. The rector there had seen our car in the parking lot and noticed our Vermont license plate. Turns out that he had been rector of a church in Vermont many years ago, and that, of course, provided an instant connection. Maybe Florida would not be so bad!

At that juncture, we still had to return to Bennington, get our house sold, make arrangements to actually buy the Whisperwood house, arrange for the moving of our household goods. All of those details yet to be accomplished. Also, Randy had not yet officially retired from Southern Vermont College and he was still employed as Organist/Choirmaster at St. Peter's Episcopal Church in Bennington.

Time always seems to drag slowly when you have major life-changing events on the horizon.

The summer of 2009 saw the final details completed. I stayed in the apartment while Randy flew to Orlando and rented a car to drive to DeLand to meet the United Van Lines movers who were transporting all our stuff! He stayed at the Whisperwood house a couple of days and then flew back to Bennington to collect me and close down the apartment. We finally packed up all the remaining stuff and the dog and took off for Florida one last time.

Arriving in DeLand, August 2010, we had lots to do to unpack our 35 years of Vermont life. I was enjoying the free-wheeling around our new house and as usual, we needed to put our mark on the house's accessibility. We have never moved without making the place more accessible than how we found it. And, as usual, Randy was unhappy with not having an organ bench to occupy on Sunday mornings. So it only took him a few days to contact the job placement listings of the American Guild of Organists Central Florida Chapter. And as usual, he was in the right place at the right time. A position had just opened at St. Peter's Episcopal Church in Lake Mary, Florida, about a 45 minute commute from our DeLand Whisperwood location. Randy immediately phoned the Rector at St, Peter's, interviews were scheduled and he was hired. Life went along for about a year or so with Randy driving to Lake Mary for rehearsals and services. But that commute on the notorious I-4 became very tiresome very fast, and we talked about another move closer to Lake Mary and Randy's job. Not much later we did just that, moving to Sanford, Florida

For me, this was a time for following some long-desired activities. I explored writing groups in Florida and found the Florida State Poets Association. There was a chapter in Daytona Beach and so I called the chapter president Bob Blenheim who told me about the FSPA Fall convention that would take place in Daytona in October. The rest is history.

I attended the convention thanks to Randy transporting me there and home. I met lovely people and shared lots of poetry. Eventually, I was elected FSPA Treasurer and Membership Chair. I had found my Florida niche.

And I was writing more and more. I entered contests and even won prizes. I was being validated and finally felt happy. I self published my first book of poetry, *In the Crayon Box, is Peace. (2012).* And after that I published *Gossamer Threads to Catch the Soul: Spiritual Reflections for the Church Year* (September 2010), which was a collection of essays I had written for the newsletter of St. Peter's, Bennington. Additional books followed: *Softness for a Hard World: Poems and Photographs,* collaborated with Kimberly Morgan Burke, photographer from Bennington; and then *Poetic Prisms, Collected Prize winning Poems,* and *Color the Sky with Morning: Poems Inspired by the Psalms* in October 2019. And still I was able to maintain mental independence and actual friendships with my poetry friends in Florida. My childhood that was primarily academic, musical, artistic, and language-based, filled with books and conversations, seemed to have been recalculating my life all along.. But I was not finished with Gertie of the GPS just yet.

On the Tip of my Tongue

Sometimes it is right there, on the tip of my tongue,
And I just can't shove it off the edge.
It hangs there with both hands
Squeezing my taste buds so hard they pop.
But the word won't come out.
All I can say is "You know, that thing that cuts the grass"
Or "that jar with the white spread for sandwiches."
I have come up with some doozies of definitions.
I have my own dictionary,
And it keeps getting bigger and bigger.
Those recalcitrant words can be so noncompliant
That sometimes I have to send them to a time-out.
Like that word for the pain in your side
 when you run too hard.
Or the word for the feeling of having been tickled too much.
And the word for the itch in the middle of your back
 that you just can't reach.
That word for the word that you cannot dislodge
From the electric misfiring of synapses and sounds.
I often think that somewhere on my tongue
There is a conference of stubborn words
 talking to each other,
And the lexicon that's used to enhance their deliberations
Would, as they say, make a sailor blush.
And the smiles continue as I search for the word
That says what I mean; you know,
That thing on the end of the hose
 where the water comes out
And the place on the cell phone that lists the people you call
And the way that the dog hops around on two legs.
And then, again, maybe there just isn't a word for that.

Maybe sometimes you just have to describe something
The way you see it. Or you just have to make up words
Like Lewis Carroll did in "Jabberwocky."
I think I'd like to gyre in this brillig day
And have a picnic of liverwurst sandwiches
And, you know, those small crispy sour things.

Chapter Sixteen
Scars and Plaques
The Worst Exacerbation

From 1985 to 2009, I was able to maintain my independence. I was working. I was driving. I was traveling. I was useful. From 1986 to 2009, as I described in prior chapters, I did have a few exacerbations of my MS: the first optic neuritis with blindness, the difficulties with walking and foot dragging resulting in using a foot orthotic, a cane and then a Canadian crutch, and eventually a manual wheelchair that I could pick up and put in my car. These difficulties seemed but bumps in the road. They were not overwhelming. I was able to continue with my usual activities. Even at home, I was able to cook, do laundry, dust, do sewing, do the things I had always done. I could take care of myself. Use the shower, wash and style my hair, use the toilet, put on make-up, get dressed.

And then, Monday, April 20, 2020, I took a shower and when I was trying to get out of the shower, my legs gave way, turning to jello that could not hold me up. I collapsed on the shower floor, imploding like a five story building being demolished for rehabilitation. My legs seemed to disintegrate under me, and I ended up crumpled on the wet floor of the shower, my legs scraped and crinkled, my left ankle starting to swell, my head dazed.

All I could do was yell "RANDY"!!!!! with all my strength. Thank God, he heard me from the other end of the house where he was practicing the organ full throttle.

As he often does, he first surveyed the situation, ignored the drama of my hysteria, and began to figure out what we could do.

"Did you hit your head?"

"No," I cried, as I lay there naked as a jaybird on the floor of the shower.

"Where does it hurt?"

"My legs, my ankle, my pride."

Then to practical matters, after realizing I did not have a concussion or an obvious broken bone, and I was not bleeding gallons, he said, "What can we do?"

"Put towels under my arm that is trying to hold up my head."

"Straighten out my legs to reduce the contortion and the pain of the twisted legs. "

The next big question was how to get me over the four inch tile barrier that separated the shower floor from the bathroom floor and kept the water contained in the shower. I am too heavy for Randy to lift me up, so that was not an option. I had to slither on my backside over the barrier without doing damage to my back or legs. Could I lift myself onto a towel that Randy could pull so I could slide over the barrier? We were grasping at straws and were willing to try anything.

Well, the "anything" was for me to slither onto a towel and to push myself and have Randy pull the towel to hoist me over the shower barrier. Once completely out of the shower and on to the bathroom floor, the next question became, could I sit up and/or stand up enough to get onto the seat of my wheelchair. My legs still felt like jello, and my arms were beginning to wear out.

We tried sliding me into the bedroom where there was a pull-down grab bar attached to the wall next to the bed. Perhaps I could pull myself up by pulling on the grab bar and Randy could slide my wheelchair under me from the back. I tried and tried. No lifting my butt off the floor, let alone getting it high enough to get the wheelchair under me. There seemed to be no way to get me off the floor and into my wheelchair. We finally decided to call 9-1-1 and ask for help from the rescue squad.

I lay on the floor, finally having a nightgown pulled over my body so I was not quite so exposed. Randy put our dog in the guest room and closed the door so she would not be so much in the way. The Fire Department is the rescue squad in Sanford so the whole neighborhood was alerted by flashing lights. Three husky EMTs arrived with equipment to take my vitals and to determine if I had broken bones or a concussion, or some kind of medical emergency that required transporting me to the hospital. No, I was okay. I just couldn't stand to get into my wheelchair. They found the best way to lift me on to the wheelchair and then to get me transferred on to the recliner chair, which Randy had prepared with a plastic sheet and several layers of towels, just in case I couldn't get up to use the bathroom.

The next day, Tuesday, I called my primary care doctor and he told me to go to the Orlando Foot and Ankle Clinic to have my left leg and ankle checked and x-rayed. That order created the next set of challenges: To get onto my wheelchair from the recliner, to use the bathroom, to get dressed, to transform myself into the semblance of a human. My ankle ached, and I was running out of self-advocacy. With the help of my walker and my husband I did finally get into the wheelchair. Randy helped me roll down our little home-made ramp from the laundry room to the garage and out to the driveway where the car was parked.

Though I had transferred a zillion times from my wheelchair to the passenger seat of the car, this morning, try as I might, I could not get my legs to hold me up enough to transfer. I tried at least 12 times before I called the ankle clinic and said we would be late to the appointment because I was having such difficulty getting into the car.

They said, "Just take your time and get here whenever you get here." With more time to try the transfer, I finally did get on the passenger seat. It only took me a total of 45 minutes and many, many tries.

We got to the ankle clinic and then there was the question of how I was going to get out of the car and onto my wheelchair. The same problem in reverse. Again, many tries. I asked Randy to go into the clinic office to see if there was someone who could come out to the car and help get me into the wheelchair. Luckily there was a technician who said he could help. So with Randy and the tech, the figuring out began. They got the wheelchair as close to the open car door as possible and with the two guys with their arms under my armpits they hoisted me onto the wheelchair. It was fairly smooth sailing from the parking lot into the clinic. I was examined while sitting in my chair. The x-ray of ankle showed a chipped bone, so the doctor prescribed a walking boot for me.

"Yeah, sure," I thought. "I can't even stand up enough to transfer. And this is a walking boot!" The irony, of course, was that I would need help from the tech and my husband to get back into the car after the clinic appointment was over. So the same thing in reverse—the two guys put their arms under my armpits and slid me into the car. My legs were still as loose as jello.

We drove home, me in tears thinking of what was to come. We got back to the house and into the driveway. Again, I could not stand enough to transfer out of the car to my wheelchair. What to do? The Rescue Squad again? Try for another 45 minutes? As luck would have it, our neighbor Antonio was out in his driveway. Randy yoo-hooed to him and asked if he could help. Thank God, he did, and I got into my wheelchair.

Back in the house. Now what? All I wanted to do was to use the bathroom and get into the recliner chair for a good rest. I'm sure you can see the handwriting on the wall??? Legs still like jelly. Could not transfer to the toilet. By this time I was in pain. We called the rescue squad again and they came again and got me on the toilet, giving me as much privacy as possible. Then they got me back in my wheel chair and then from there on to the recliner chair. And that is where I stayed for seven days.

I was devastated. How could this be happening to me, Mrs. Independence!!! My body felt bruised and battered. My psyche was destroyed. After 35 years of relative independence, living with my MS diagnosis, my world stopped turning. I was shattered. I was vulnerable. I was dependent. I couldn't even brush my teeth without help. My legs were so weak that I could not transfer from one seat to another. I spent seven days living in my recliner chair in our living room with a plastic sheet over the chair. I was relegated to using incontinence supplies. The realization that this MS thing was not so easy anymore just about fried my brain. I could not see myself as a worthwhile person any more. How can you see yourself as worthy when you are peeing on towels in your living room, when you cannot get yourself a glass of water in the kitchen, when you cannot get up to answer the doorbell, when you are completely dependent on another person for survival. My face was often wet from weeping. My eyes, puffy from crying, were often just slits in my face.

Finally, on Thursday, I called my neurologist and asked what I could do, whether I was eligible for any Home Health services. Having lived in Vermont and worked for the Vermont Center for Independent Living, I was familiar with services for people with disabilities available in Vermont. Florida was a new beast. But my doctor got me set up with a home health agency that would come to my home and offer nursing care, occupational therapy, physical therapy, and medical social work assistance, along with a hospital bed and a hoyer lift. I am one of the lucky ones with Medicare and good medical insurance that would cover the cost of the services.

The hospital bed and the hoyer lift were delivered on Saturday, April 25. Randy and I had tried to figure out where the best place in the house was to put the hospital bed. Because I could not imagine when I was going to be involved in crafts and card-making again anytime soon, we figured the hospital bed should go in my craft room. That room is at the back of the house next to the screened porch and right off the dining room. After living in the recliner chair in the living room for seven days, I was looking forward to a change of scene and a bed. Randy rearranged furniture and craft "stuff" in what would become my new bedroom. There was space for the hospital bed and the lift. Now the only thing left was for me to get there.

Home Health services began on April 27 with a visit from the physical therapist Ellen. She was wonderful. That first visit was spent figuring out a way to get me into my wheelchair from the recliner chair where I had spent the last week. We tried several strategies, using my walker for stability and the recliner chair to lift me up to a more vertical position. After a few tries, and combating my fear of falling, I finally got into the wheelchair. The next task was figuring out how I could get onto the hospital bed in my new bedroom. Ellen and Randy figured that if they could get the bed as low as possible, and get me lined up right next to the bed, they could sort of lift and roll me from the wheelchair on to the bed. It worked, but imagine a 100-pound sack of potatoes being maneuvered by two children. You get the idea of what they were up against. Once I was splattered onto the bed, I burst out in tears of relief. Oh, my God, we did it! Next was getting me centered on the bed and discussing what the next steps would be.

Ellen had an excellent PT regimen for me, to strengthen my legs and to work toward being able to get out of bed using my walker for stability and pivoting to sit in my wheelchair. No more heave ho's to get me into bed. I had a lot of work to do!

My sense of loss was starting to take hold. What more could I lose? I had lost the ability to use the toilet and take a shower. Ellen tried to be my cheerleader. You can do it. Small steps. Be satisfied with tiny improvements. As I was struggling with my MS exacerbation, the world outside was struggling with the Covid pandemic. As housebound as I was, the pandemic was not affecting my hopes to be out and around, to go out to dinner, to go to church. I felt so bad for my husband who had become my caregiver in every sense of that word. He cooked, did laundry, changed me, cleaned me up. We certainly became closer than ever before. I was stuck in bed for nearly eight months. Then, because of a urinary tract infection, I had a great deal of bleeding. My primary care doctor and my neurologist said I needed to find a urologist to figure out what was causing such massive bleeding.

I was lucky to find a doctor that I felt comfortable with and who was able to perform the test needed to come to a diagnosis. The doctor determined that I had a massive bladder tumor which was causing the bleeding and discomfort. I underwent a cystoscopy and the bladder tumor was removed. The doctor showed me pictures of the tumor that he said was the size of an orange. After the pathology report came back, I was so relieved to learn that the tumor was benign and I did not have bladder cancer.

But that is not the last of the 2021 exacerbation. Yes, you may say, what else could go wrong. Well, MS is a strange disease and presents many, many twists and turns. The next adventure was another fall in the bathroom. Trying to rise from the toilet with the help of my walker, again my legs gave way and down I went. Another adventure — this time Randy used the hoyer lift to raise me from the floor of the bathroom and transport me to my hospital bed. A call to my neurologist got me a bed at Advent Health Orlando hospital. There I underwent a series of tests to see how active my MS was and if there were other issues affecting my strength and endurance. A full body MRI, many x-rays, blood tests, urinalysis, and many others tests were performed, which took three days. At the end of the diagnostic testing, the results showed that I had many MS lesions, many of them quite old but a few active and inflamed. I also had a spinal fracture that was almost totally healed. I also had a 4cm mass on my right kidney.

What next? I had 18 days in the Inpatient Rehab facility of the Advent Health Winter Park hospital. In order to be admitted to that facility you have to show that you can handle a six hour daily regimen of all sorts of therapy — physical therapy, occupational therapy, speech therapy, recreational therapy, and more. At Rehab I was introduced to my new best friend. Her name is Sara Steady. She is a device that has allowed me to stand up from bed or other seat and then be rolled to another seat in another place. I never thought I would be able to stand again, but Sara proved me wrong. Admittedly, I am not independent and Sara has to be placed in front of me and someone has to adjust the seating flaps and roll me to a designated landing place. But let me tell you, it is lots better that falling.

And also there is the mass on my right kidney. That was cancerous and the entire kidney had to be removed. The doctor said that there is no metastasis and I will not need chemo or radiation after the kidney is removed. My kidney surgery, a radical nephrectomy, was scheduled for Thursday, August 26, 2021.

And after all that, we come to the episode of kidney stones in October 2021. I was in such pain, that Randy called 9-1-1. The EMTs came and got me into the ambulance and transported me to the Florida Regional Hospital in Sanford. There the ER doctor ordered a CT scan of my abdomen and took my history. When I told him I had had a radical nephrectomy of the right kidney with Dr. Cohen in Winter Park, the ER doc phoned Dr. Cohen to tell him that I had a massive kidney stone in the left kidney, my only remaining working kidney. Dr. Cohen told him to get me into an ambulance and to send me directly to the Operating Room at Advent Winter Park Hospital where he would meet me.

After another cystoscopy and the insertion of a stent to allow for the passing of the kidney stone, the terrible pain subsided a bit. After three days in the hospital I was sent home with instructions to call Dr. Cohen regarding the removal of the surgical staples and further information about home health care.

And this, my dear readers, is why I am a person of hope, of light, of gratitude, of sunbeams, of the benefits of recalculating. I am convinced that there will come a time when I will graduate from wearing nightgowns all day to wearing regular street clothes, and a time when my husband and I will reach our 50th wedding anniversary together.

What You Never Remember

There is no memory of the prickers
In the garden as you find the gooseberries
Or when you look for hidden apple falls
Where the tree has died.

Your recall is thwarted when it comes to locating
The scent of lemon clover
Or whiff of damp soil in the field
That was last tilled where the earth is fresh

You cannot recall how the lilacs drooped
Their lavender arms across the brick
Walkway under the kitchen window
And how the back garden
Was always ablaze with tea roses
Perfuming the air in July
And how the scent of flour seeped
Into your dress when your grandmother
Baked bread in the oversized kitchen
In the house on Bowen Street where
The stove had a creamy enamel finish on pendant handles.

It's hard to retain the harsh sound of
The front door slamming as the wind
Blows it hard into the door frame
Or the grating sound of pebbles thrust
Against the side of the house
Before a thunderstorm began.

What you never remember are the things
You don't want to forget.
How the bird feeder
Outside the kitchen window is full
Of bluejays and sparrows all winter long
As the mourning doves collect
The seed droppings below the feeder.

How the cat kneads her paws
On your stomach,
And how soft is the pillow on your bed
When you bury your face in its comfort.
And you just can't remember what he said to you
When he left the house with his suitcase
On that chill December afternoon.
You know it was important,
But you just can't remember.